Learn How to Draw Computer Portraits for the Beginner

Step By Step Guide to Drawing Portraits Using SAI Paint Tool

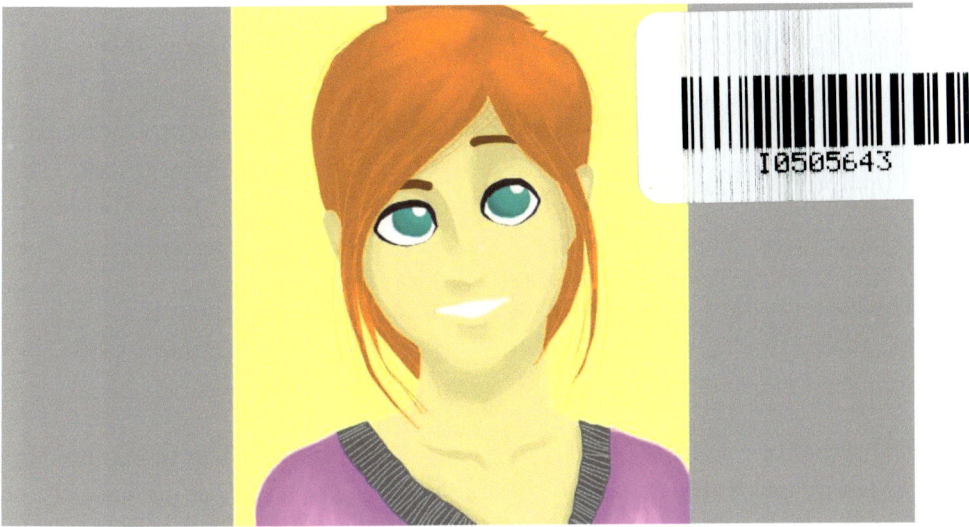

Learn to Draw Series

Rosselle Taruc

Mendon Cottage Books

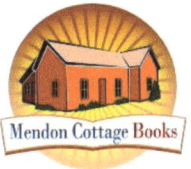

JD-Biz Publishing

Disclaimer

The information is this book is provided for informational purposes only. It is not intended to be used and medical advice or a substitute for proper medical treatment by a qualified health care provider. The information is believed to be accurate as presented based on research by the author.

The contents have not been evaluated by the U.S. Food and Drug Administration or any other Government or Health Organization and the contents in this book are not to be used to treat cure or prevent disease.

The author or publisher is not responsible for the use or safety of any diet, procedure, or treatment mentioned in this book. The author or publisher is not responsible for errors or omissions that may exist.

Warning

The Book is for informational purposes only and before taking on any diet, treatment, or medical procedure, it is recommended to consult with your primary health care provider.

Our books are available at
1. Amazon.com
2. Barnes and Noble
3. Itunes
4. Kobo
5. Smashwords
6. Google Play Books

Table of Contents

Introduction 4

    What do I need to start? 4

    How do I acquire SAI Paint Tool? 4

The Drafting Process 8

The Coloring Process 20

Author Bio 55

Publisher 58

Introduction

Digital drawing is a lot easier than how most people presume it would be. Sure, nothing beats drawing the "old school" way but we have to admit, and you will see soon enough, that drawing digitally has its own share of perks as well.

This tutorial will guide you through making your own digital art. With easy-to-follow instructions from drafting, outlining, and coloring, this is the tutorial perfect for those who are just being introduced to drawing digitally.

What do I need to start?

I have been using SAI Paint Tool ever since I owned my drawing tablet. It is light software with UI that is direct to the point, as well as, containing all the basic tools a digital artist may need. SAI is the perfect drawing software for those who are still new to the digital art world. But, the software is not for beginners alone--countless renowned digital artists have also favored using SAI, and we will see the reason why pretty soon.

Preferably, what is recommended to use, is an actual drawing tablet and its pen, rather than using a mouse. Though you can still go on with just the latter, it will definitely take more time and feel less "natural" than when you're actually doing art on a drawing tablet.

How do I acquire SAI Paint Tool?

SAI can be downloaded for a free 31-day trial period at this link: http://www.systemax.jp/en/sai/

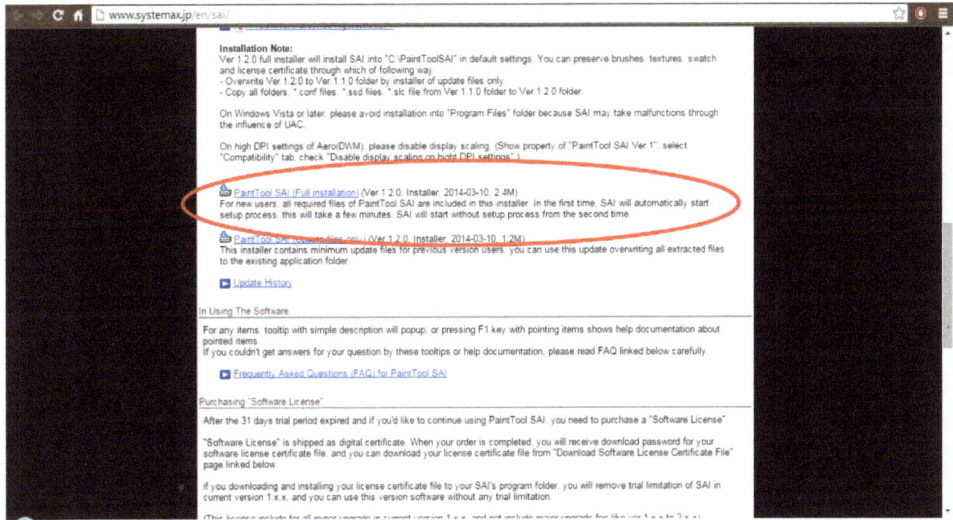

Installing the software is very easy. Once you click the encircled link, and it has finished downloading, click on the obtained file and a User Account Control dialogue will pop up. Click "Yes" and the installation dialogue will appear, as shown below.

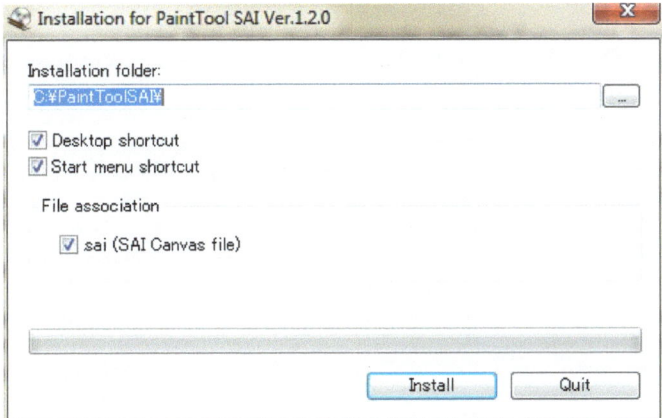

Click "Install" and the installation process will begin. After a few seconds, a dialogue will appear that the installation was successful, and you can finally use the software.

Click on the launcher to begin.

In this tutorial, for the sake of clarity, I have shifted the location of the tools and the layers, as well as removed some of the color palette tools so that the whole setup does not look so crowded. To follow what the setup in this tutorial is, simply click on the "Window" tab and copy what is checked and unchecked below.

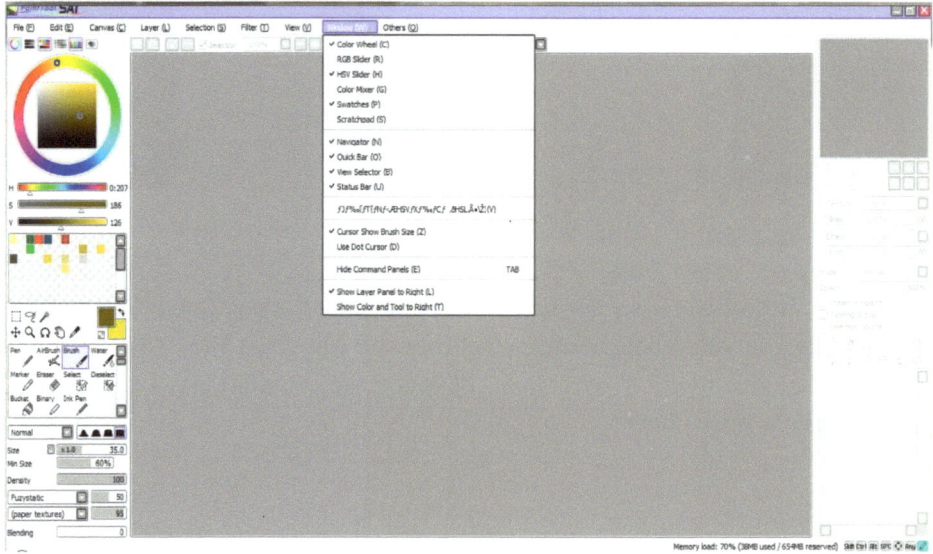

Now, this tutorial will tackle the draft process, the utilization of SAI's Linework feature, coloring process, as well as, applying some effects to the illustration. Note that the whole coloring process does not necessarily have to be in the order of what will be on the step-by-step procedure. Remember that this tutorial is only a guide to helping you get to know *digital drawing* and that there's a lot more to discover and experiment on the software.

It goes without saying, the drawing, and coloring style of each individual vary, so do not hesitate to deviate from what is only seen on this tutorial.

On deciding what to draw: inspiration is everywhere! From your classmate, your sibling, that funny-looking couple you saw on the train, your favorite fictional character, that person who appeared in your dream last night, or even what you think the neighborhood cat would look like when transformed into a person, there are endless possibilities to what you can draw. And that's the beauty of it. Let your imagination soar, and let it soar high.

From being inspired from real-world experiences to being inspired on what you saw on the internet, relieve your artistic itch, and let's begin!

The Drafting Process

1. Open SAI Paint Tool.

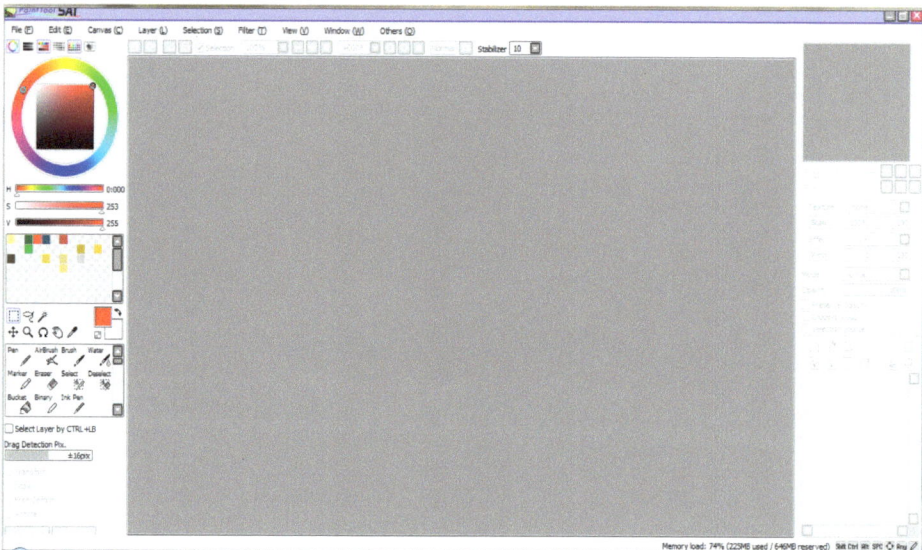

2. Click "File" and select "New".

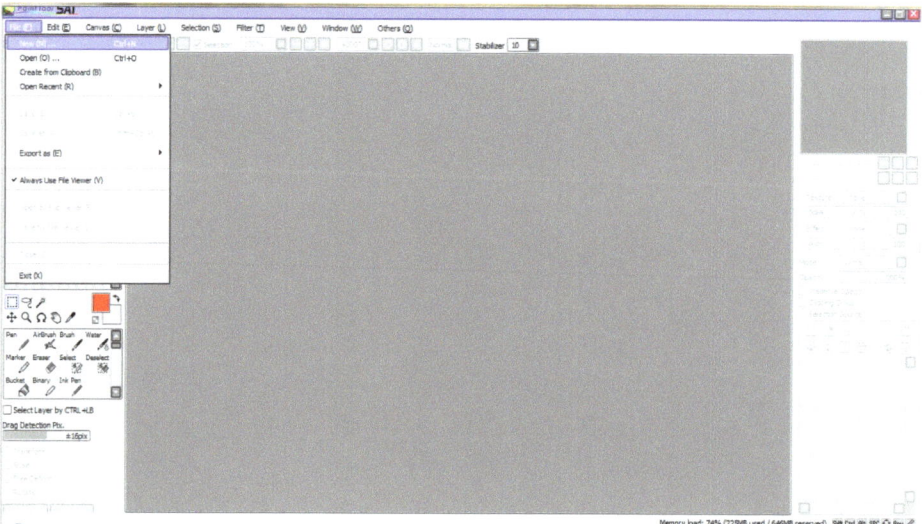

3. Select a preset. Remember that you can always change the size and resolution midway.

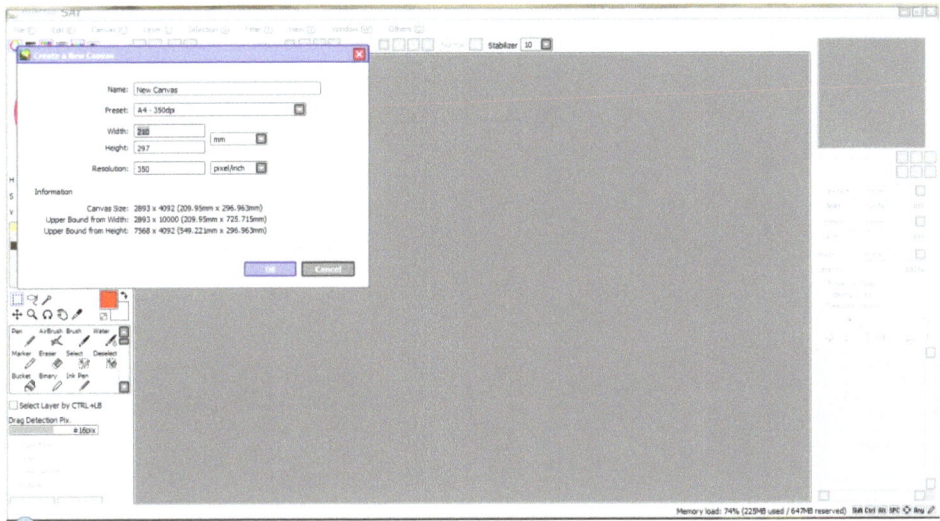

4. After clicking "OK", you are now presented with a blank canvas. You will see that "Layer 1" automatically gets in the Layers section (lower right part).

5. The first thing to do is to draw a draft. However, before you proceed, it is very important to rename "Layer 1" with what you want you want to label your draft. This is because layering is an essential part of drawing digitally. Therefore, as you progress in making your art, it is inevitable that you will have multiple layers. To avoid confusion, renaming each layer before you draw on them is highly recommended. Do this by double-clicking on the said layer. A popup will then appear.

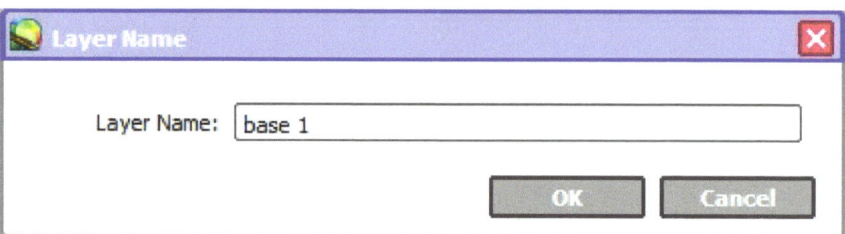

Type whatever you want to label your draft layer and click "OK" to proceed.

6. Now, it's time to finally draw. For this, the Pencil/Pen tool is almost always used, and it's found on the opposite side of the layers section. It is recommended to use a very vibrant, distinguishable color. Bright shades of purple, blue, or red are mostly used in this. You will see shortly as to why this is recommended as we proceed.

Don't be too wary of making mistakes. Remember that there is always the Eraser tool which can also be found on the tools section. Also, you can always access the Undo command by pressing "Ctrl"+"Z".

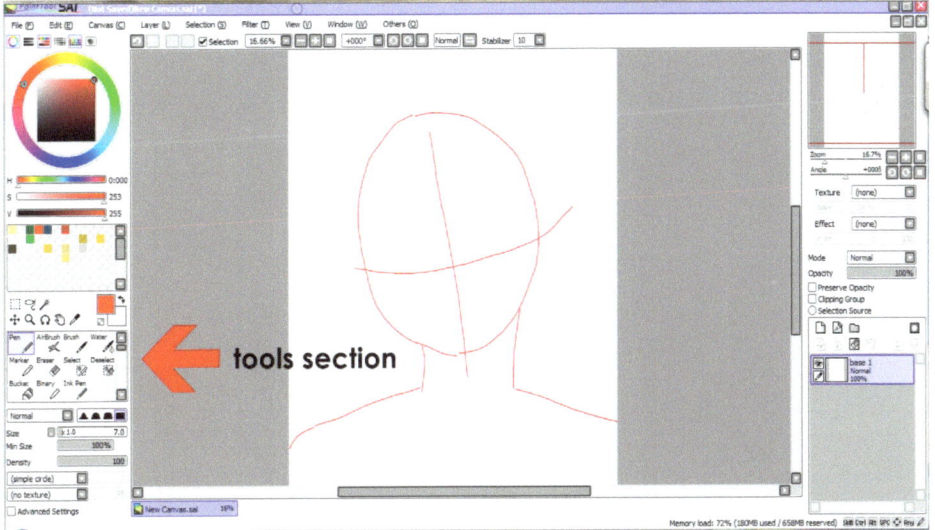

tools section

7. Now that I have the main structure of the illustration, it's now time to draw a much detailed draft. Before proceeding, make a new layer and rename it to however you want to label the draft. To create a new layer, click on the blank page icon located above the layers section.

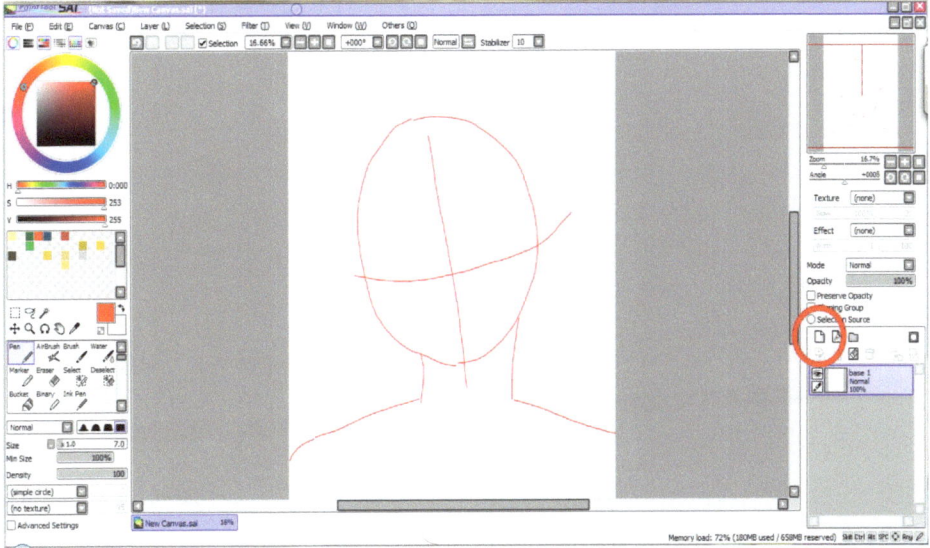

A new layer will appear, named "Layer 1" by default. Repeat the renaming process as mentioned before. I have named mine "face base" since it will contain the facial features.

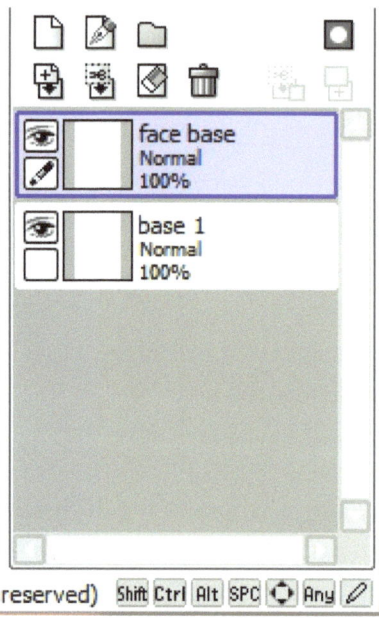

Segregating the content of each layer is very crucial because doing so will lessen the risk of losing previously-drawn content. To illustrate, click on the new layer.

Notice that when the new layer is selected, using the eraser tool on the content drawn on the previous layer does absolutely nothing. This is because creating a layer is like creating a protective barrier. Only what you put within the said layer can be manipulated, therefore securing whatever content you have drawn on previous layers.

Now, the next thing to do is put this new layer, in this case my "face base" layer, **above** the previous base layer. I will do this by dragging the desired layer on top of the "base 1" layer.

You might be asking, "Why do I need to bother with the positioning of the layers?" When dealing with just lines, and no solid objects whatsoever, the positioning of layers does not seem to be that important. However, when you start utilizing solid objects, that's where the position, or more specifically, the order of the layers play a very important role.

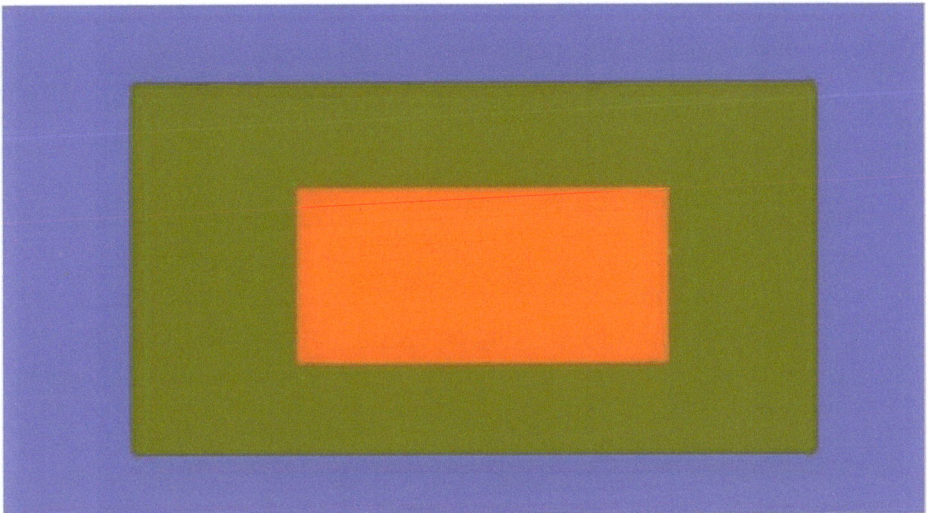

To illustrate the concept of the importance of layering order, assume that the picture above is what your eyes can see on the canvas, the **eye-level** view.

However, this picture below is how the **top view** looks. The yellow circle represents the viewer's line of vision. That is, what is put on the topmost layer gets to be seen readily, overlapping whatever that is below it.

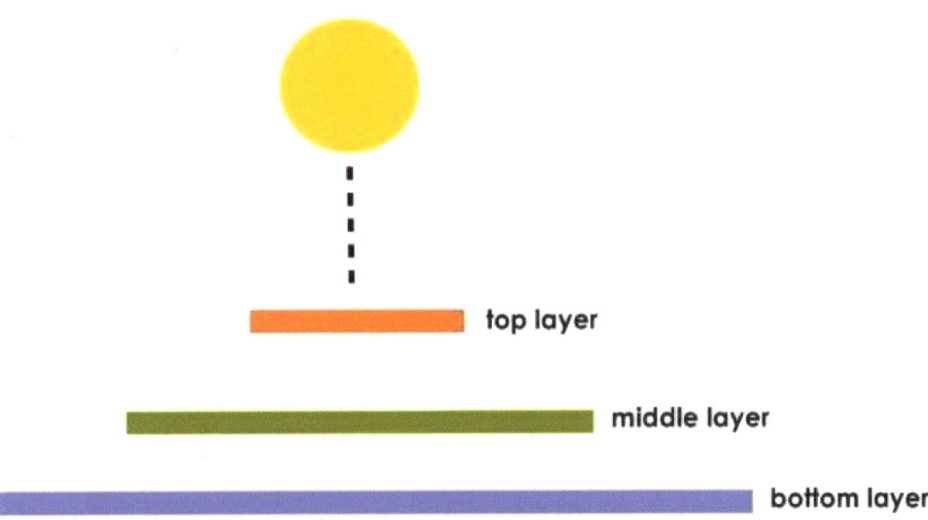

Let's say that the green object gets to be put on the topmost layer instead of the shorter orange one, the result is that what would be seen on the **eye-level**

angle would merely be an indigo rectangle containing a green rectangle--the latter completely hiding the orange rectangle from sight.

Now that that is cleared up, let's move on to drawing features on our illustration.

8. Before drawing anything, make sure that you're drawing on the correct layer. In this case, I should be drawing on the "face base" layer by clicking it. You may have noticed that the canvas is tilted to the right. You can achieve this by clicking on the tilt button, as encircled below. To the left of this buttons is where the zoom buttons are placed, marked with + and - icons.

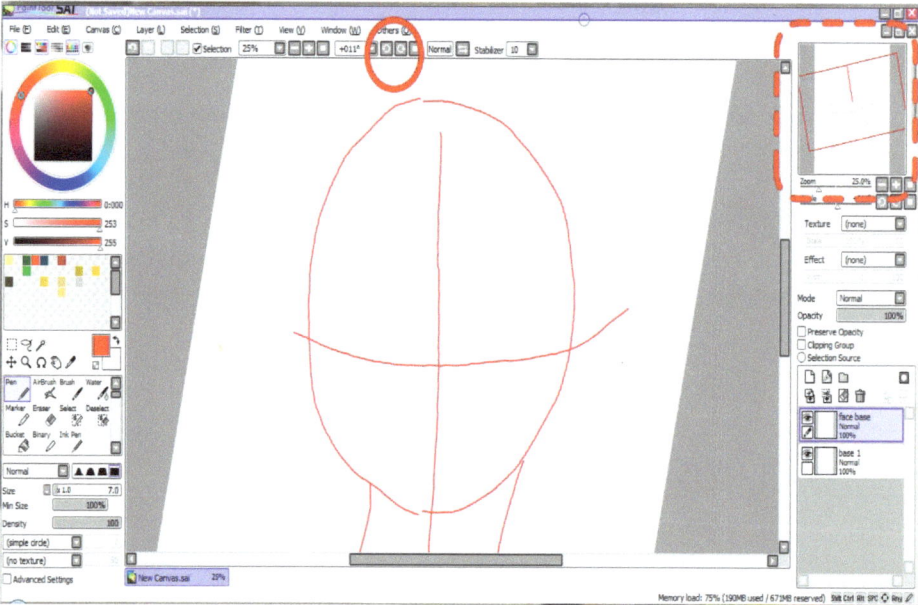

9. Now that I have finished drawing the facial features of my subject, the next step would be to draw the shape of the face, neck, and upper body. In short, I'm going to work on the whole area where skin is involved.

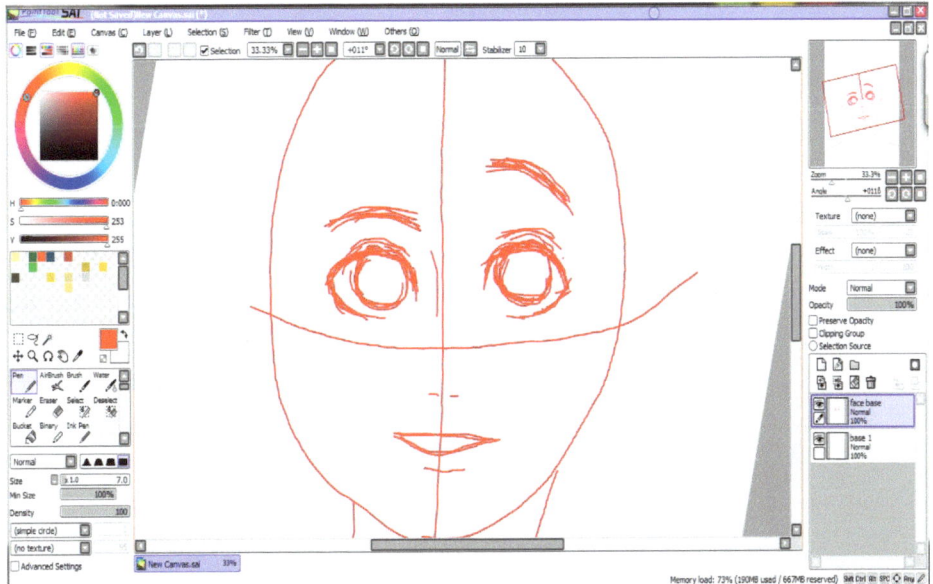

10. Again, I make a new layer and rename it "skin base." I drag this on top of the layer where the facial features are.

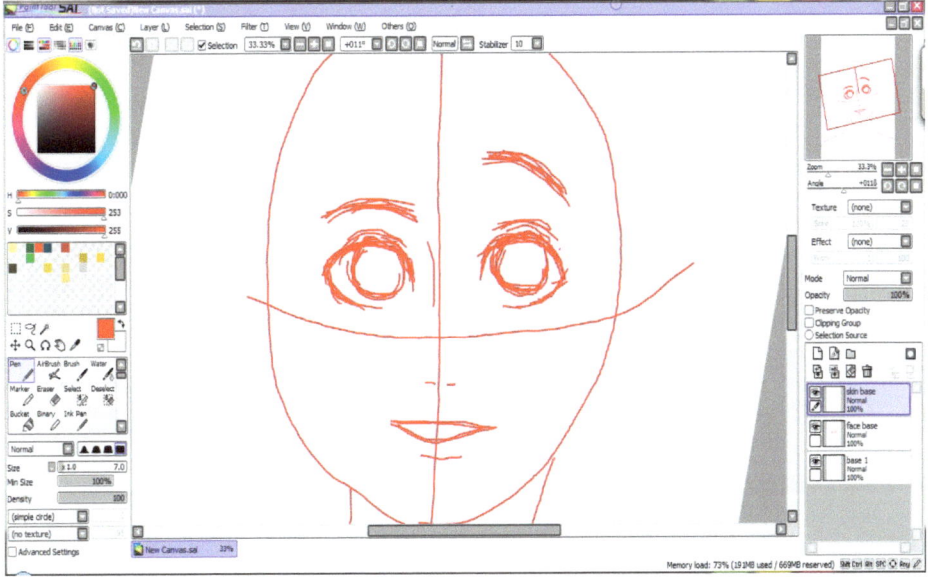

11. Now that I have finished that, it's now time to draw the hair.

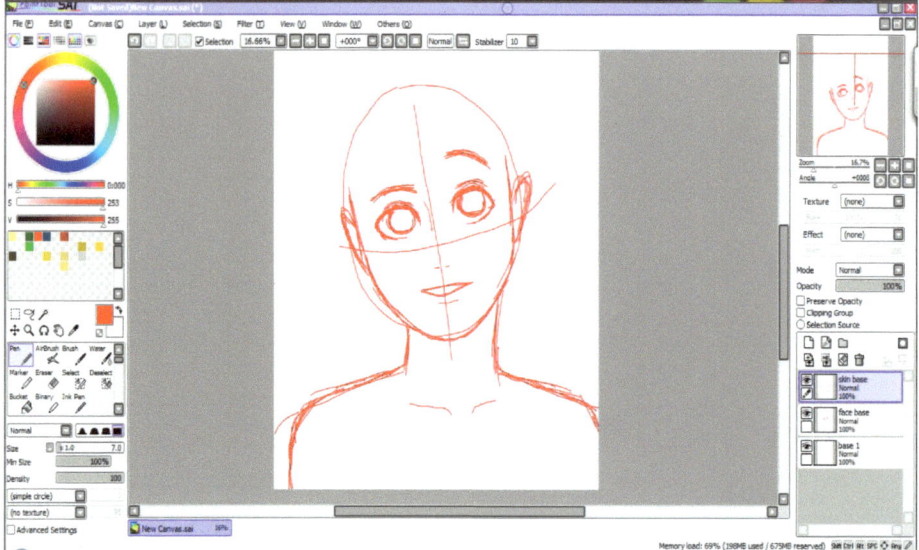

12. I make a new layer and name it "hair base." Again, I've put this at the topmost position.

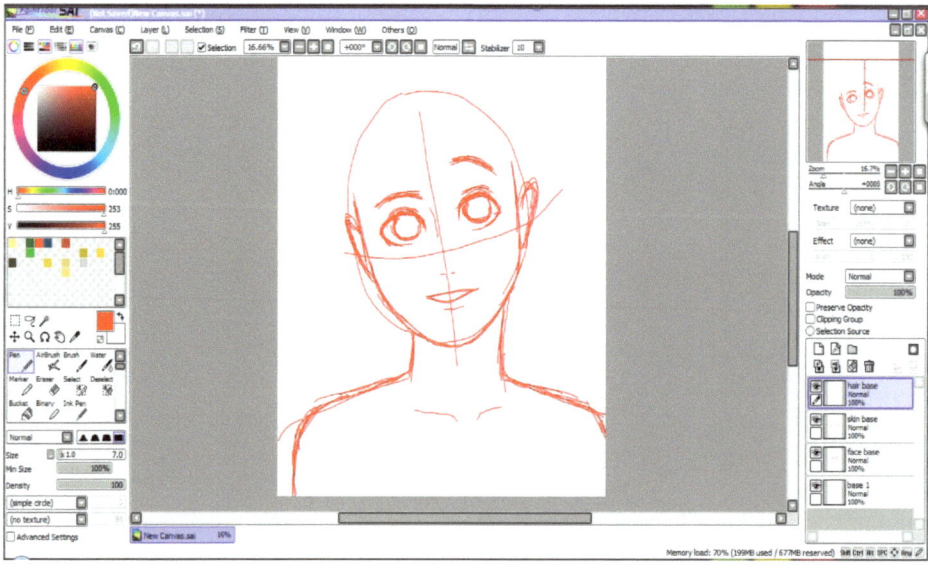

13. Hair is done; the last thing left to draw is her clothes.

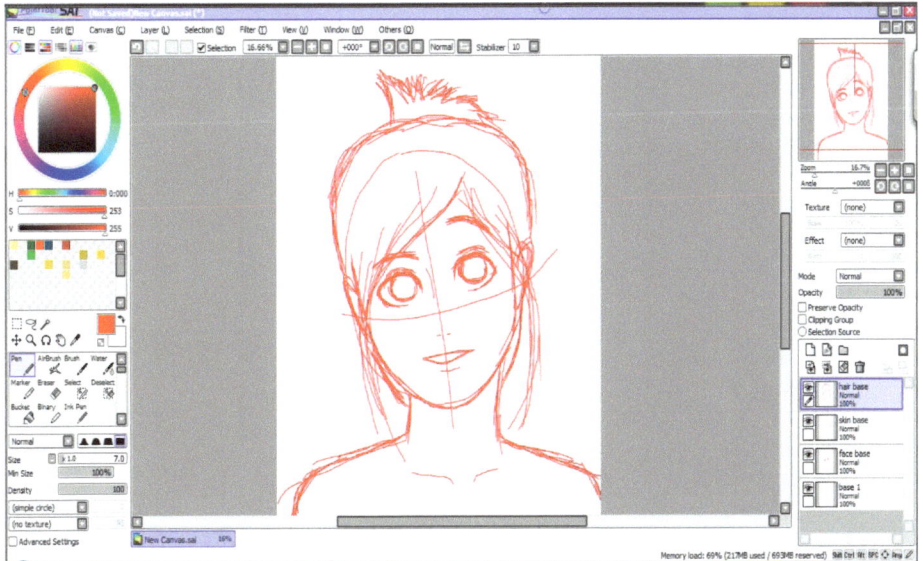

14. Always, always remember to do the "new-layer-rename" process before proceeding to actually draw. Let that be your mantra throughout the digital drawing process. By adding the clothes, I have now finished drawing the whole guide.

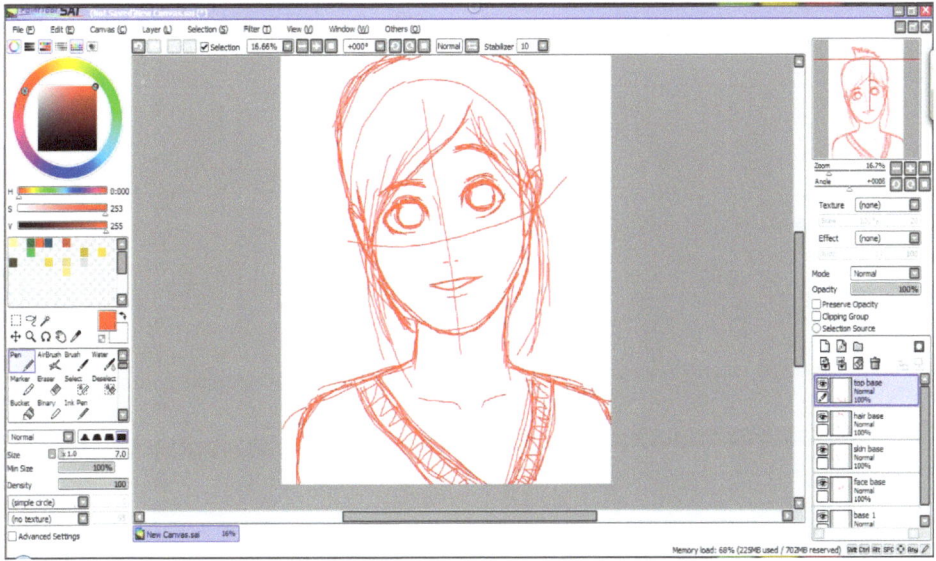

15. Once you are satisfied with your draft, merge down all the layers to compile them. The "Merge Down Layer" button is located at the layers section, as highlighted in the picture below. Remember, once you have

merged down a layer with what's at the bottom of it, editing it would be a lot harder since the contents are no longer segregated from one another.

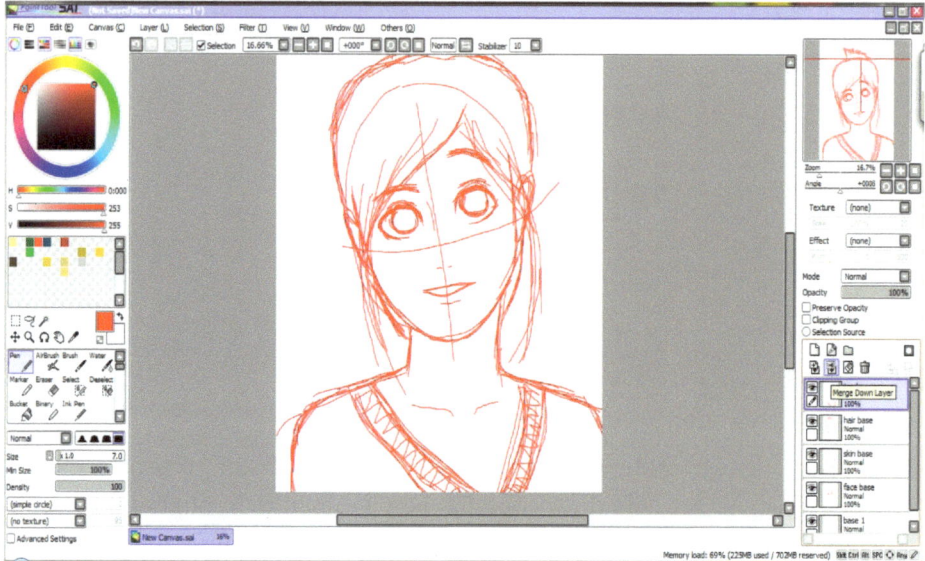

16. Now, put the main guide at the very top of the layers section, since you will need to see this almost throughout the coloring process.

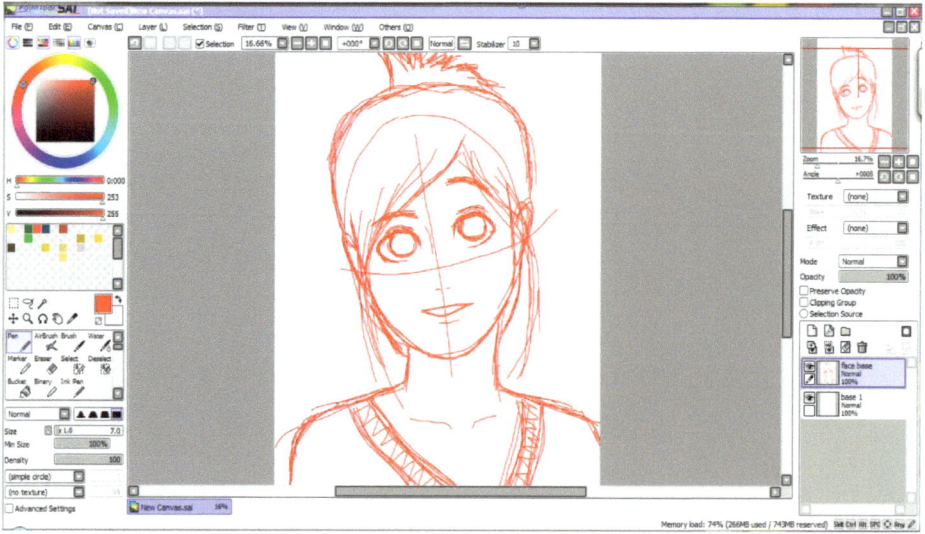

17. Dispose of the empty layers by pressing the "Delete Layer" button which is, again, located at the layers section, as highlighted below. This

is done to make the layers section free from clutter. I will delete the "base 1" layer since I no longer feel it is necessary. Remember that whenever you make a mistake, just press the Undo command.

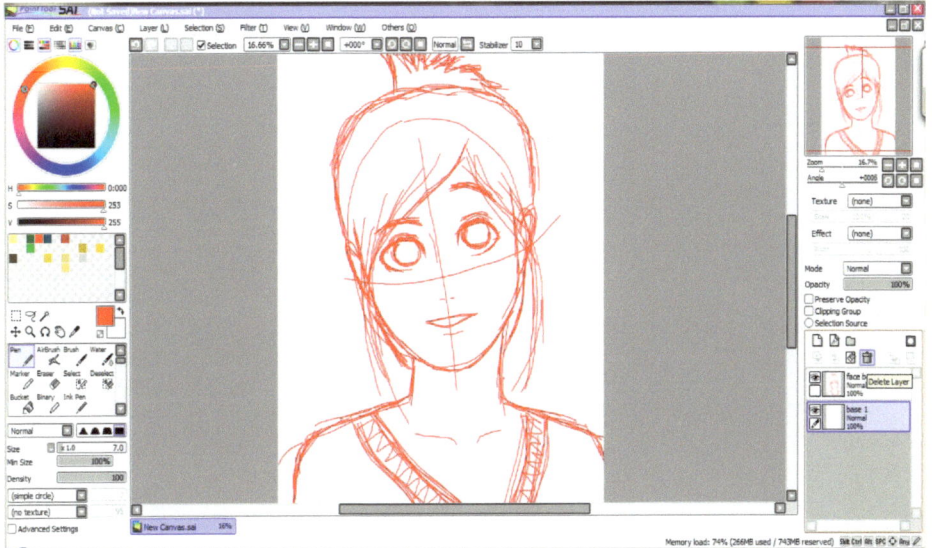

The Coloring Process

We are now officially through with the guide-making process! Now comes the fun part: Coloring.

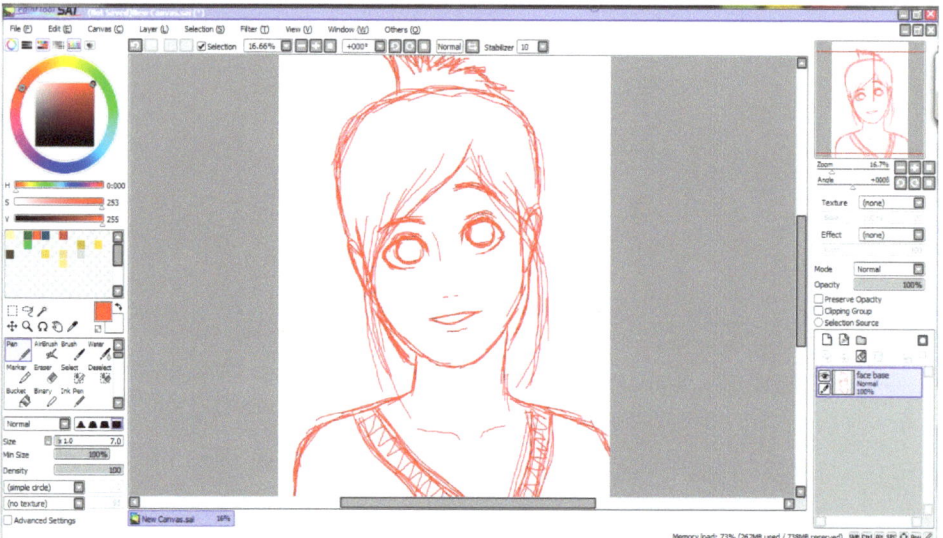

1. Before proceeding to making the final outlining, it is highly recommended that you lower the opacity of the layer containing the draft. To do this, simply click on the opacity scale above the layers section, as encircled below. Since the whole guide is drawn in red, this will greatly help in not making you confused as to which line is which as you start to color. Add the lowered opacity and you will surely have no trouble distinguishing which is the guide from the new lines you are going to make.

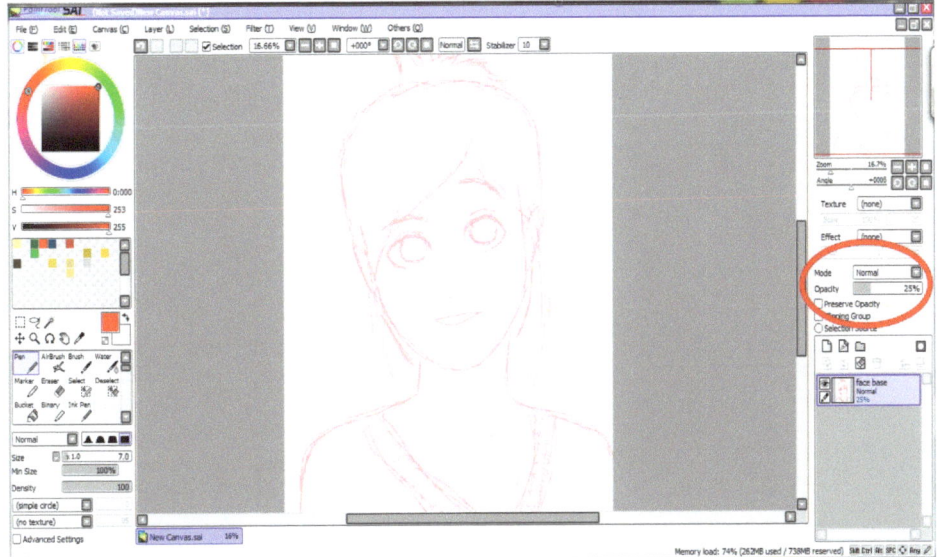

2. From here on out, every layer that will be made should be **under the layer containing the draft**.

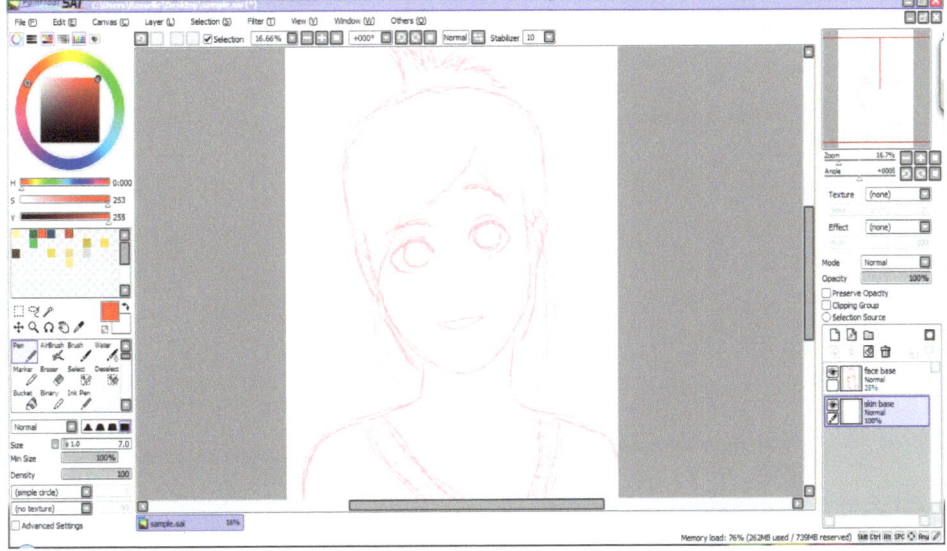

3. Now, what we want to do is provide the color for the skin. I'm going to use the same Pen/Pencil tool. This time, enlarge the size of the Pen so as to make the coloring process faster. Do this by clicking the down arrow on the "Size" as highlighted below. Pick out the most appropriate size for the illustration. Remember that unlike "tangible" drawing, there are

several ways to completely avoid out-of-bound coloring in digital illustrations. So there is little need for coloring very precisely.

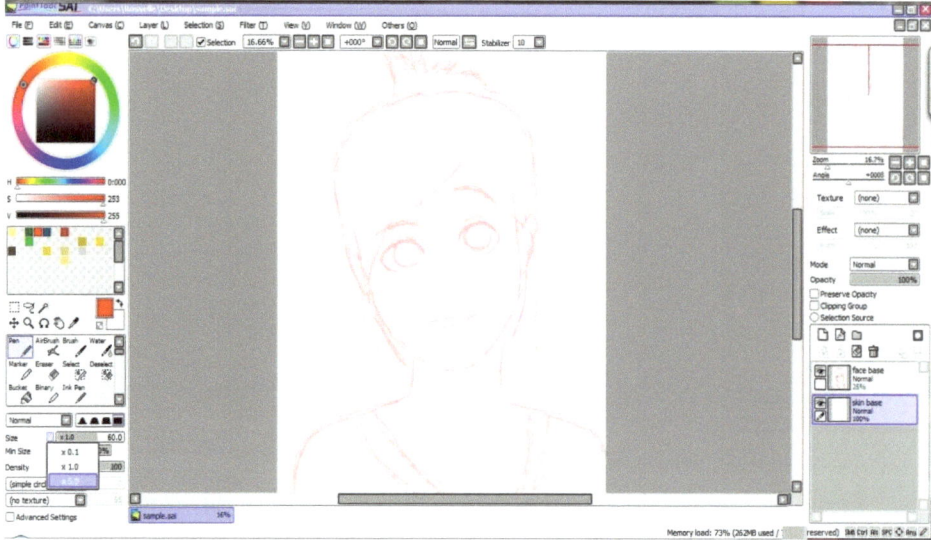

4. Don't worry about the very messy coloring; the next step will be to clean out all of the excess colors with the help of a very useful, SAI-exclusive tool.

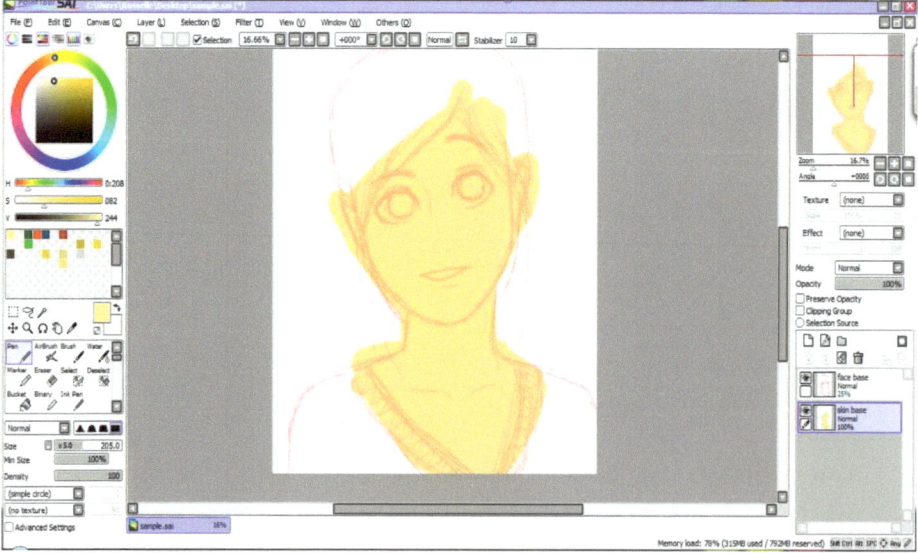

5. We start by making a new "Linework Layer." To do this, click on the button highlighted below. A new layer will appear, only this time it has

---

this pen icon next to the thumbnail. Notice how when you click on this layer, the tools on the tools section almost completely gets replaced with new ones. Again, don't forget to rename every new layer you're working on.

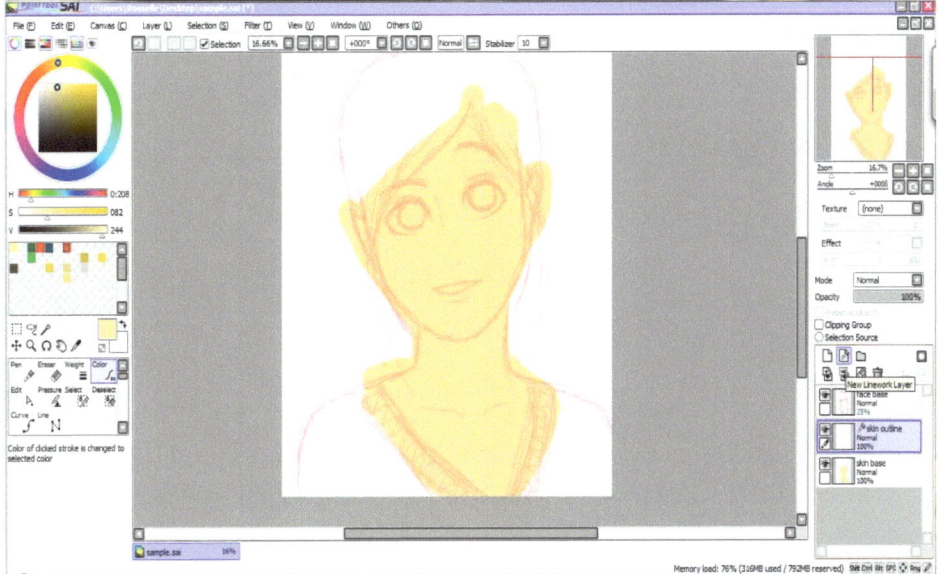

6. You will see soon enough what differentiates a Linework layer from an ordinary layer. To get to that point, let's first use the Pen tool to make the outline of what we're going to color in. Again, use a distinguishable color, like bright blue or purple. I'm going to use green. One major advantage of using a Linework layer is that you can edit the lines you draw very easily, so don't worry too much on making a mistake--even the colors of the line can be changed very quickly, too.

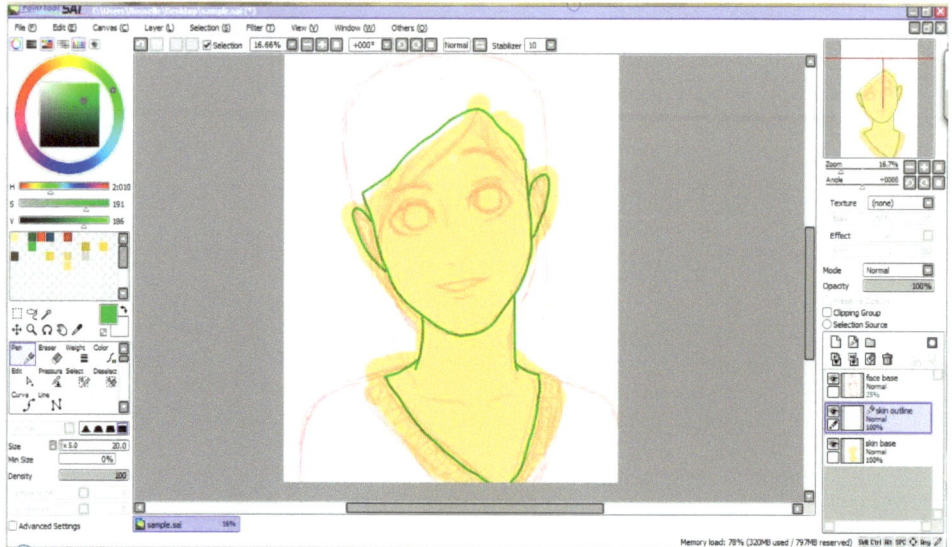

7. Once I have finished the outline, it's now time to use the Edit tool to straighten or smooth the lines I've made. This is as easy as dragging the points you put your cursor in, and making it go whichever way you want.

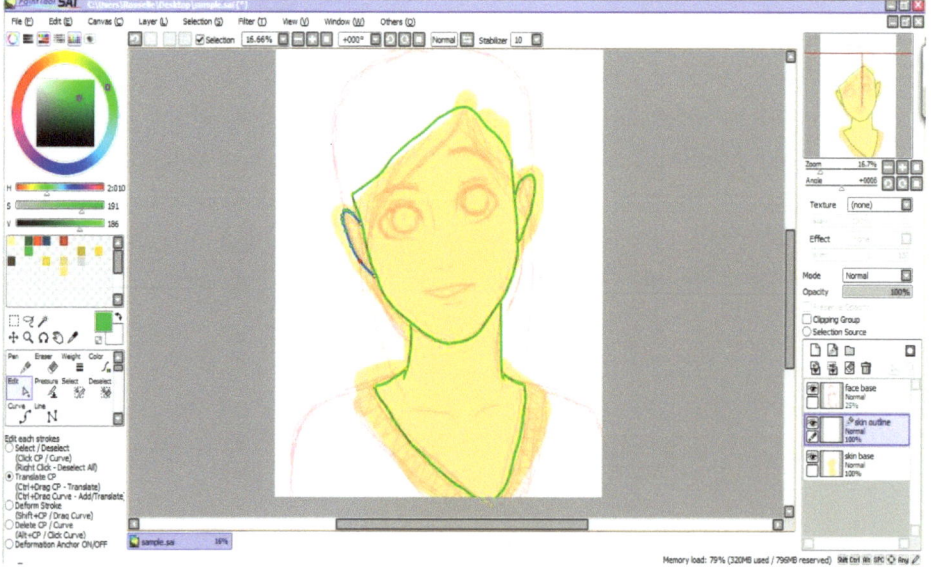

8. BEFORE EDIT TOOL: notice how squiggly the lower part of the ear is. Also, the line on the upper part of the face does not meet the line at the

top of it. Remember that a Linework almost always has to be a **closed figure** in order for the "cutting" of excess color to work.

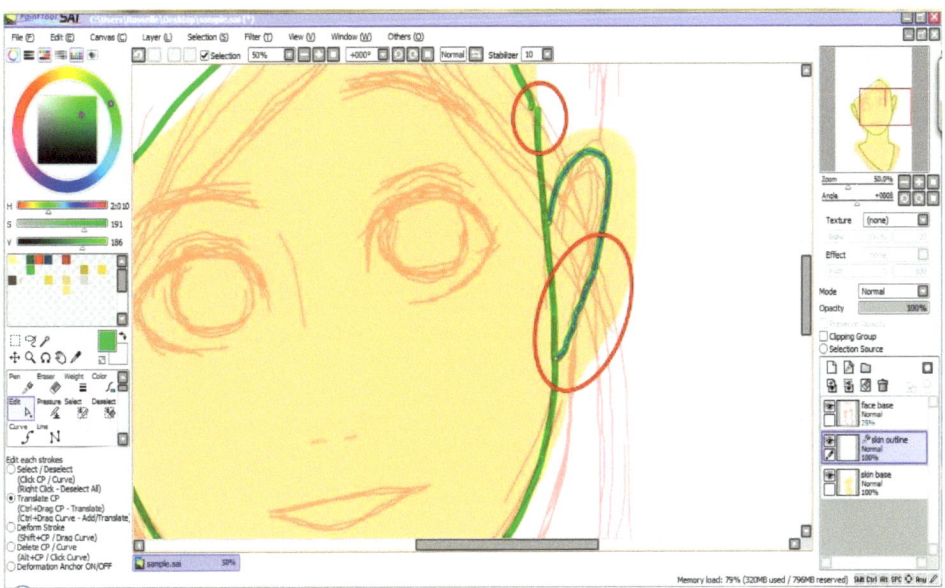

9. AFTER EDIT TOOL: See the corrections made simply by dragging the highlighted point on the direction you want it to go.

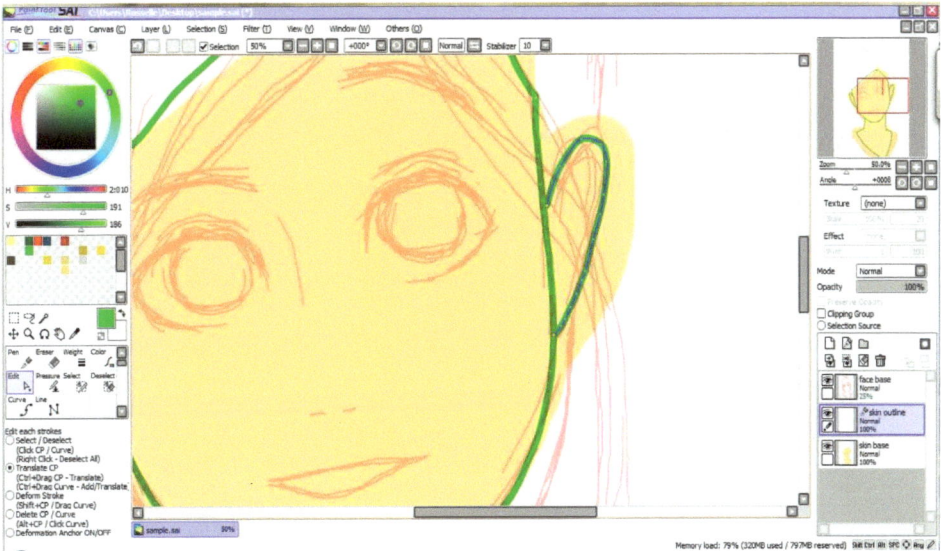

10. Now, when you're satisfied with your outline, as well as certain that it is a completely closed figure, click on the Magic Wand tool located above the tools section, as highlighted below.

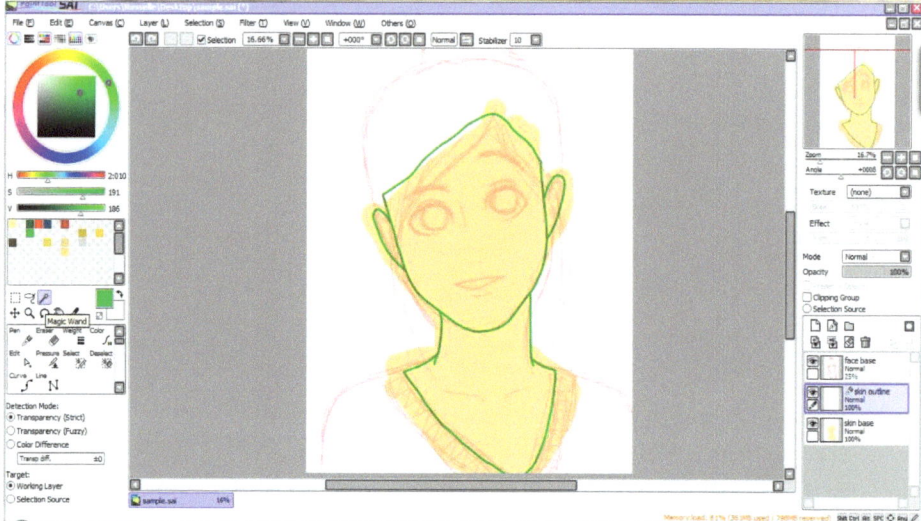

11. Click on the area you want to clean out. Notice how the enclosed portion gets filled by blue, this just means that that part is highlighted. It does not affect the color of the illustration.

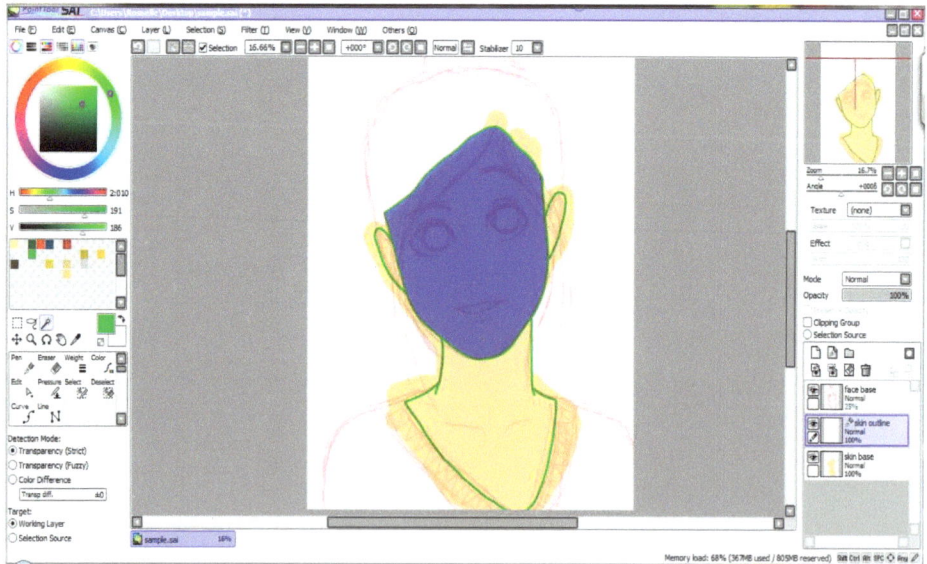

12. I continue clicking on other areas I want to clean out.

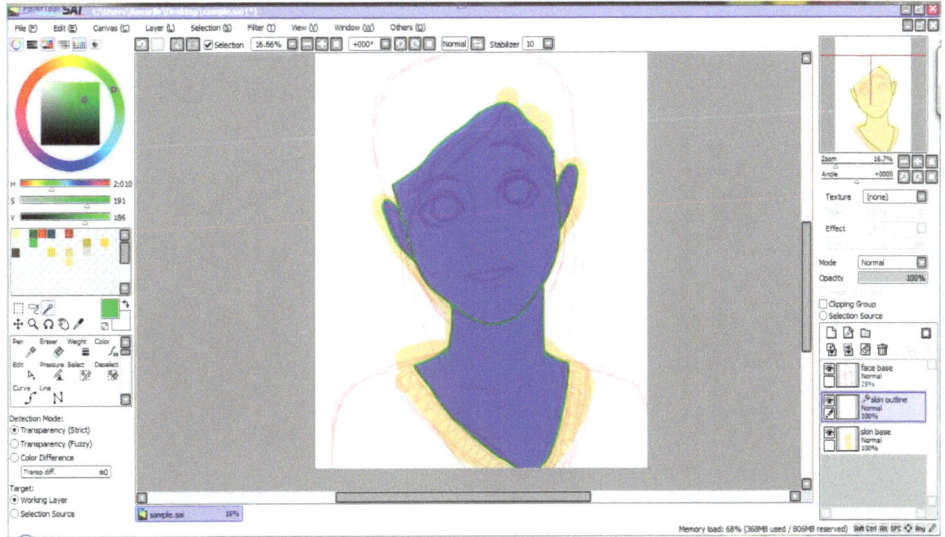

13. Next, once I have highlighted all the area I want to clean, I click on the "Selection" tab and select "Invert."

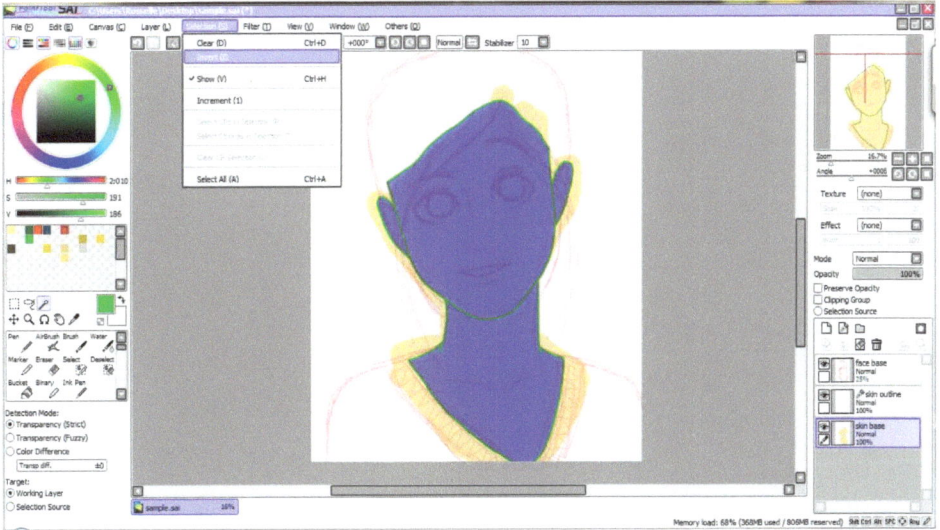

14. Doing so will highlight what's outside of the face--that is, where the excess colors are. Now, I click on the layer where the coloring of the skin is. By highlighting an area, it means that only that selected portion can be manipulated, and nothing else. By doing this to my illustration, I'm ensuring that the inside of the skin area does not get manipulated.

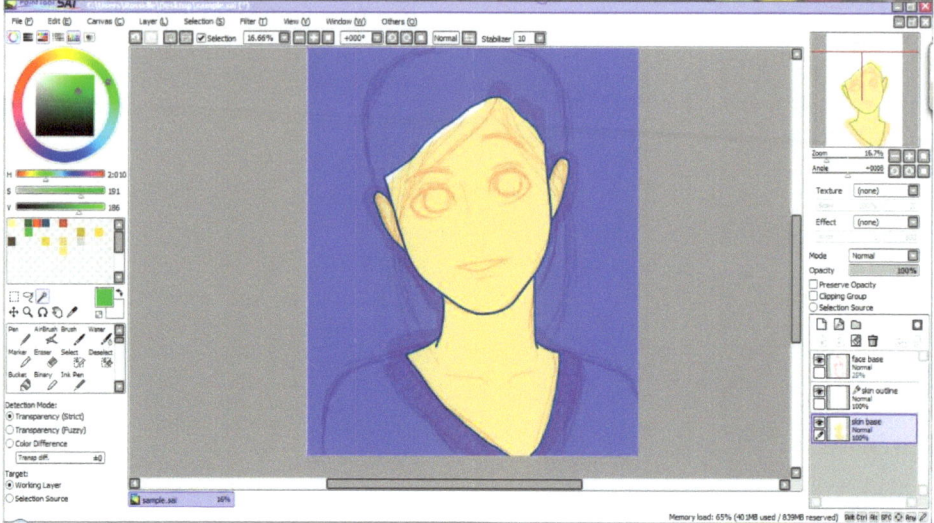

15. Next, I click on the Eraser tool. Notice how when you select a tool from the normal layer, the blue highlight goes away, only to be replaced by moving broken lines.

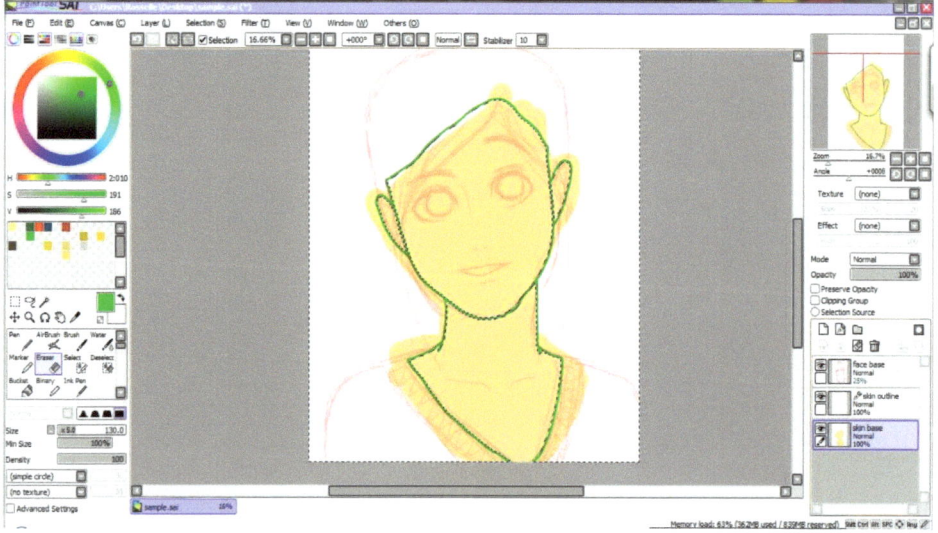

16. I start to delete the excess colors. This is how the "precise" coloring looks like.

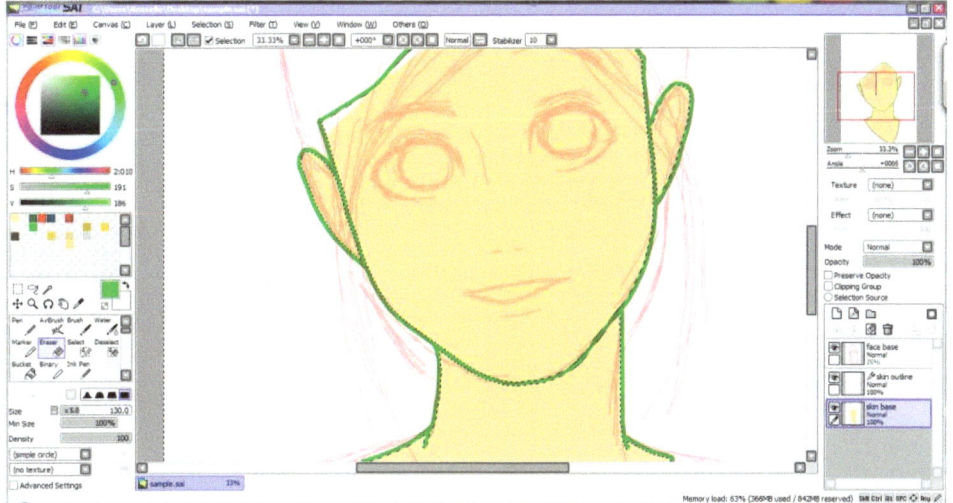

17. Next, I remove the highlight by clicking on the "Selection" tab once more and selecting "Clear" or by just simply pressing "Ctrl" + "D".

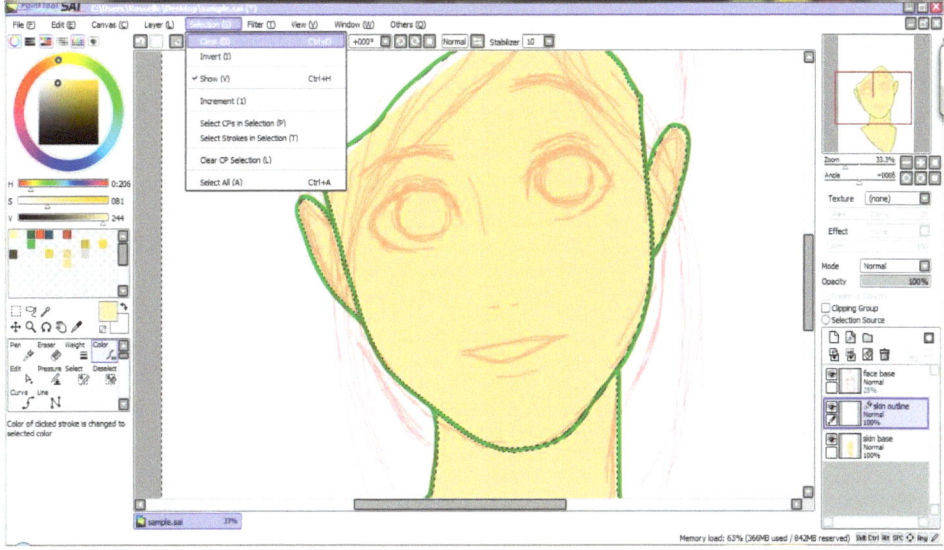

18. Next thing to do is to change the color of the outline, which is green at the moment. I do this by selecting on the Linework layer where I have made the outline of the skin and choose the Color tool. You change the color of a line by simply clicking on it while the desired color is selected from the color palette.

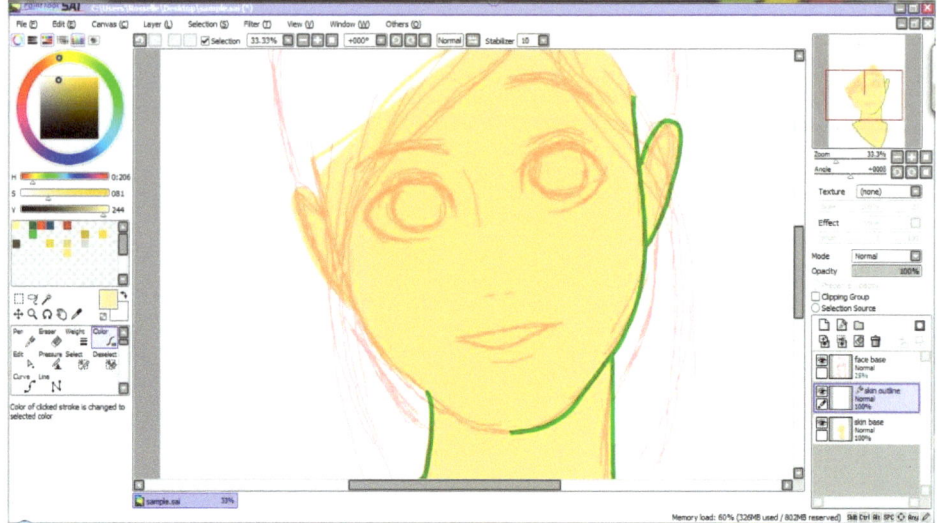

19. This is how the finished base color of the skin looks like.

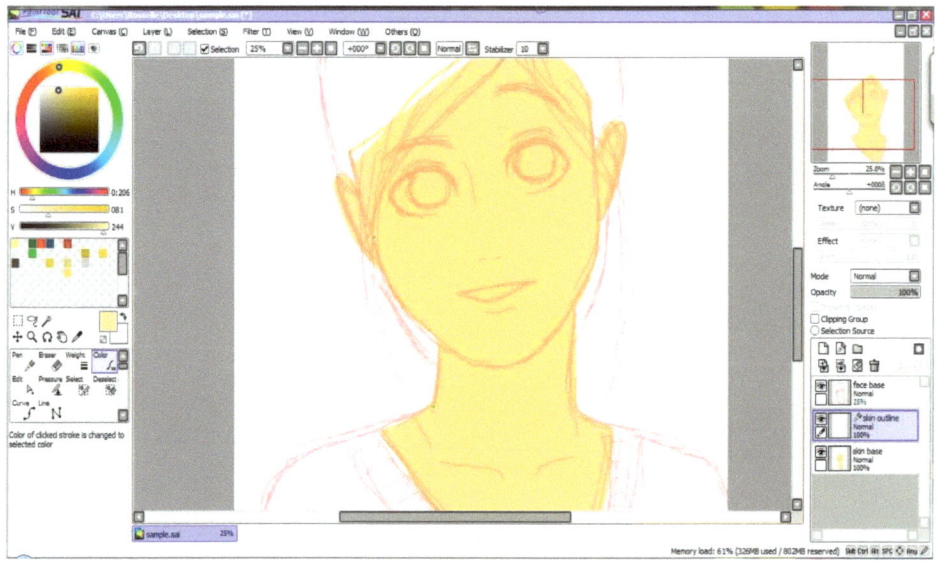

20. Next, we color the hair. First, make a new layer for where you would put the base color for the hair. Remember to put this layer **above** the skin layer.

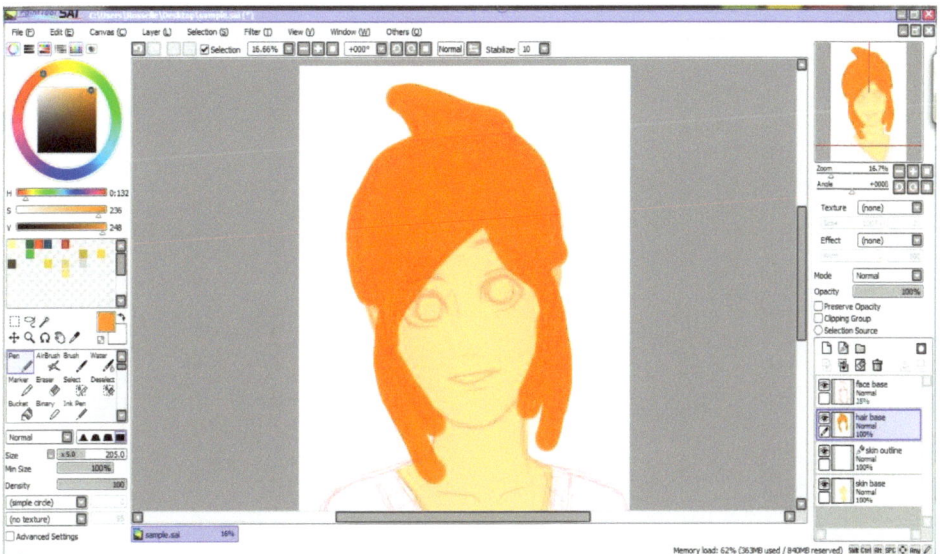

21. We make another Linework layer, and proceed to make the boundary for the hair.

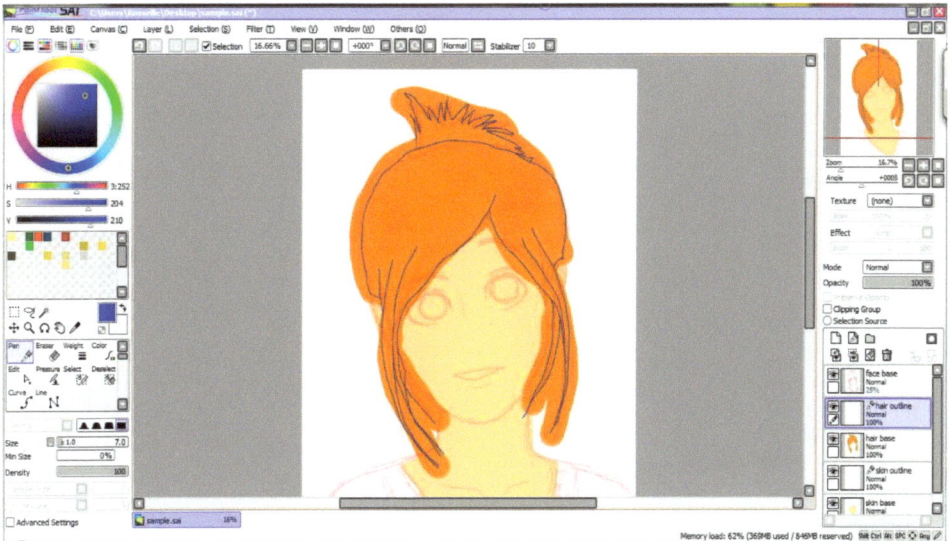

22. We do the editing process once more, ensuring that the Linework is a completely closed figure. This time I use a bright blue color for the Pen tool.

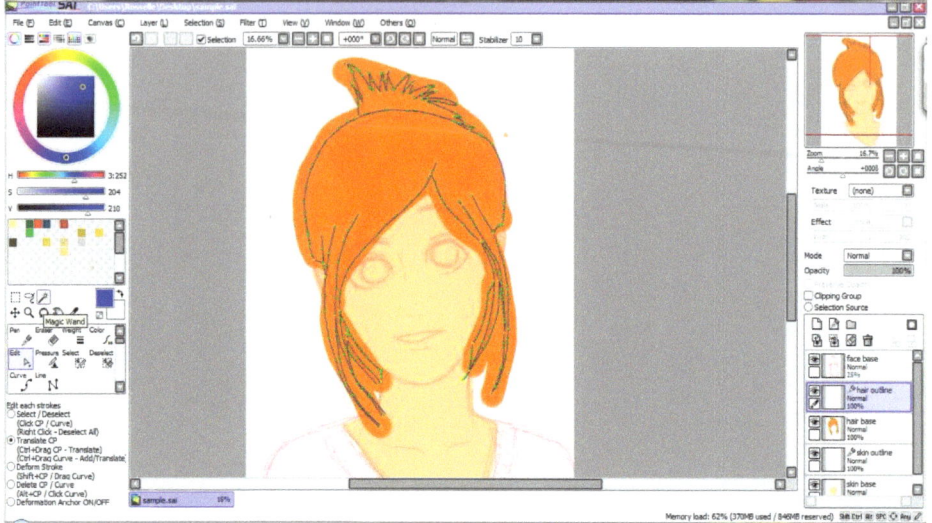

23. Use the Magic Wand tool once more, selecting the hair area.

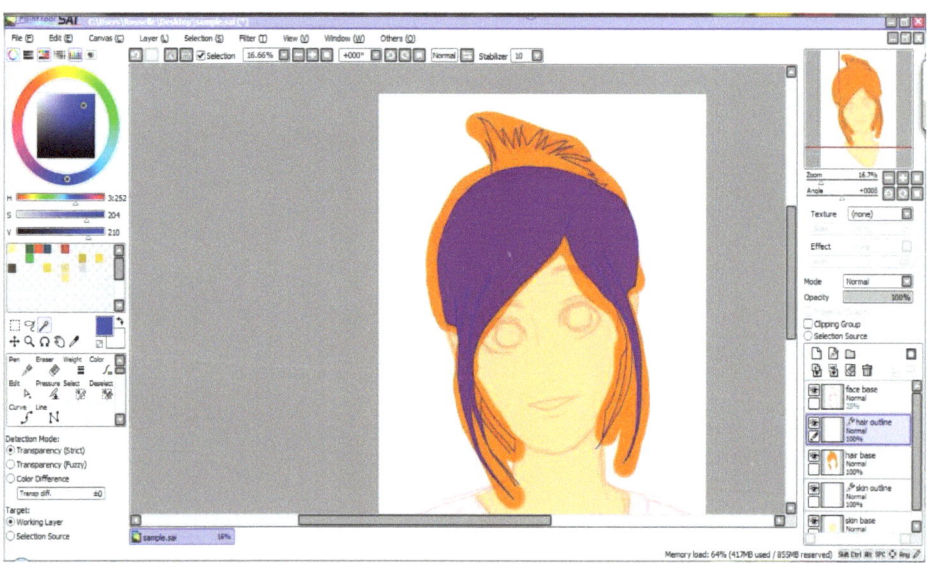

24. This is what how the hair looks like when completely highlighted.

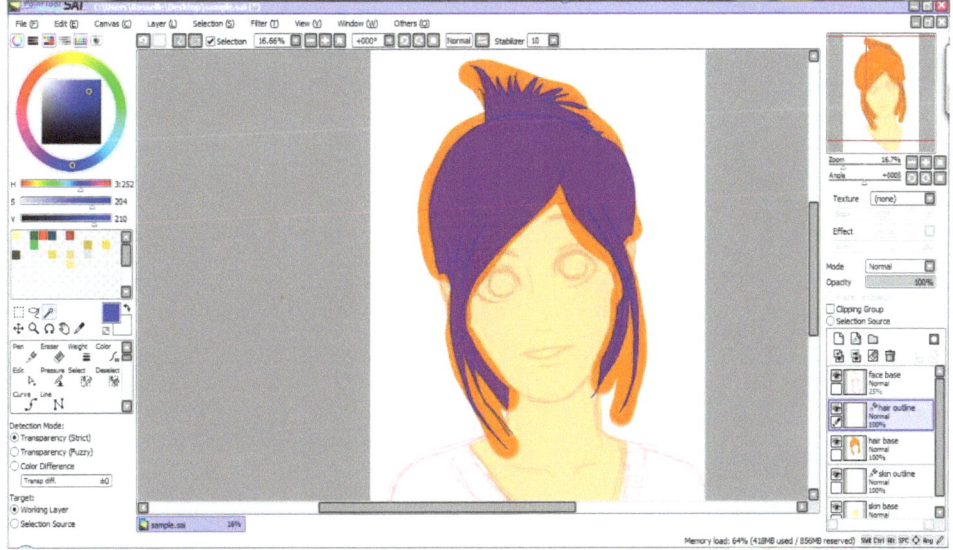

25. We click on the layer where the coloring of the hair is, and proceed to invert the selection before erasing excess colors.

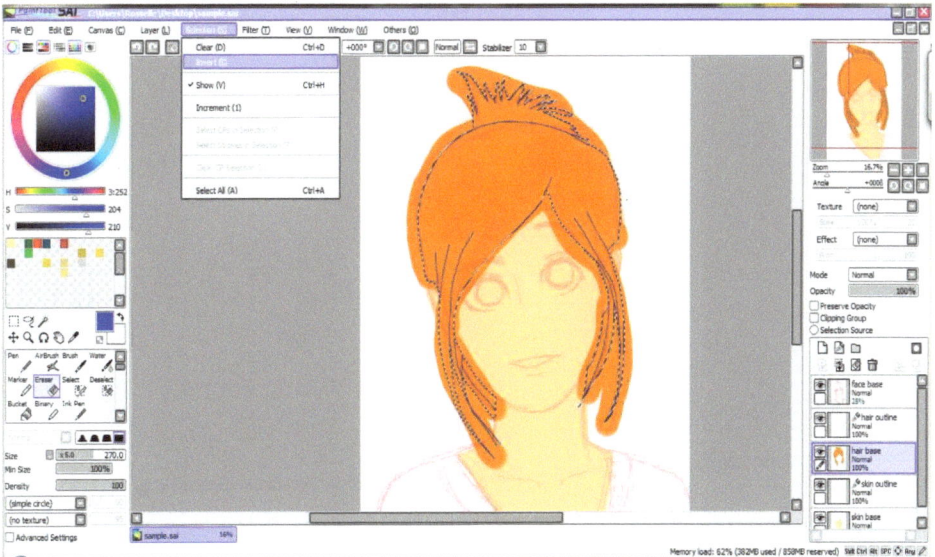

26. This is how the hair looks like when the excess color is removed.

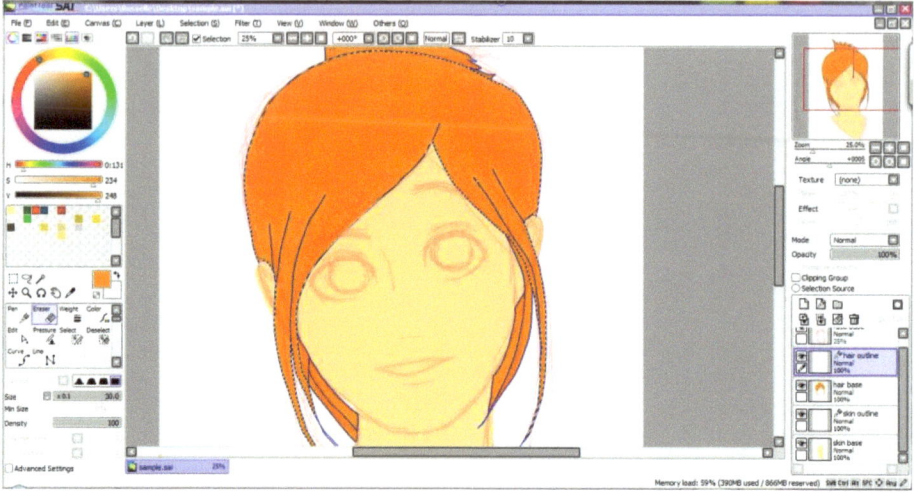

27. Now I will change the color of the Linework. To do this, I click on the Linework layer and select the Color tool.

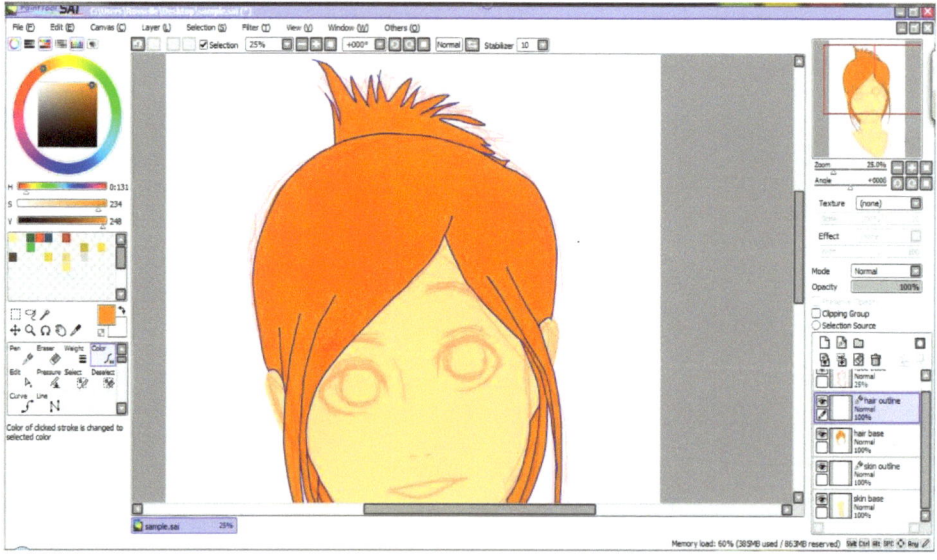

28. I choose the same color that I used for the hair and click on the lines.

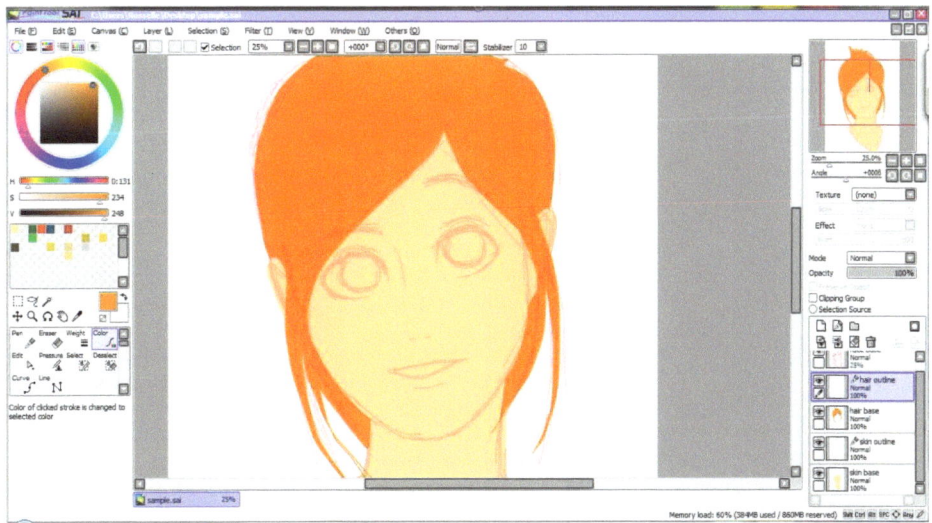

29. Now that the hair and skin are done, we move on to the face area. We make another Linework layer to make an outline. Remember to use the appropriate sizes of the Pen tool when lining, use thick sizes on features that should be easily seen, and thin sizes for the more subtle parts.

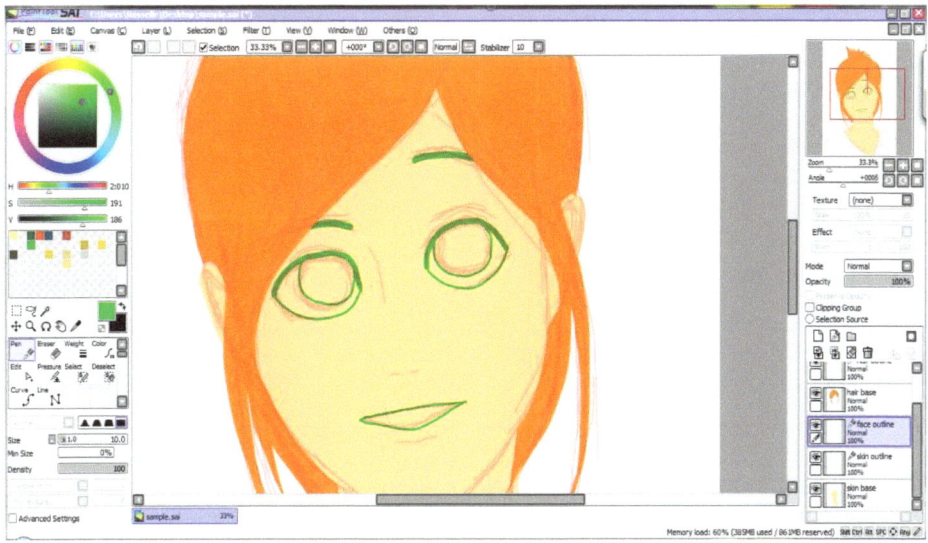

30. Another great feature of Linework is that by using the Pressure tool, you can adjust the thickness of each point on each line. Those green dots that you see are the adjustable points that can be made thin or thick by this helpful tool.

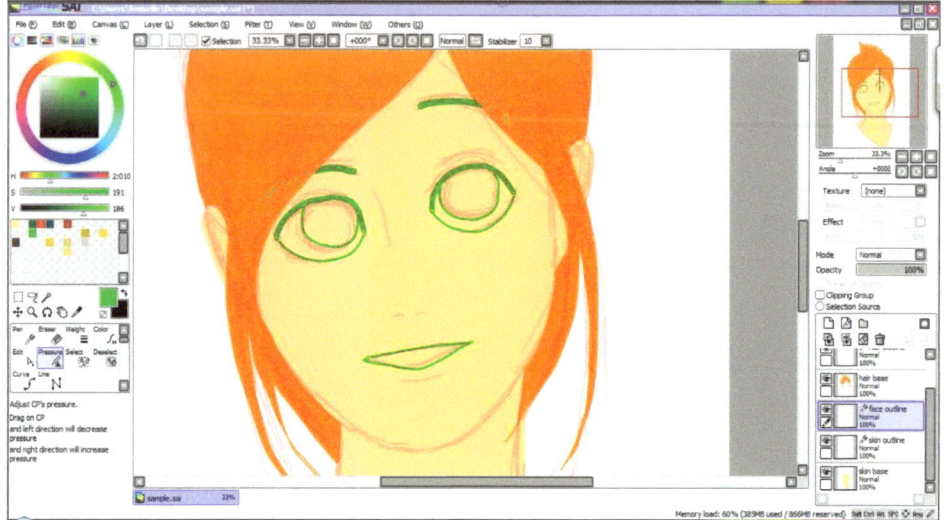

31. To make a segment of a line thick, simply click on the desired point and drag the cursor to the **right**. If you want to make a segment thinner, click on the desired point and drag the cursor to the **left**. You can only double the thinness or thickness of a line, so make sure you use the appropriate size of the Pen tool when lining.

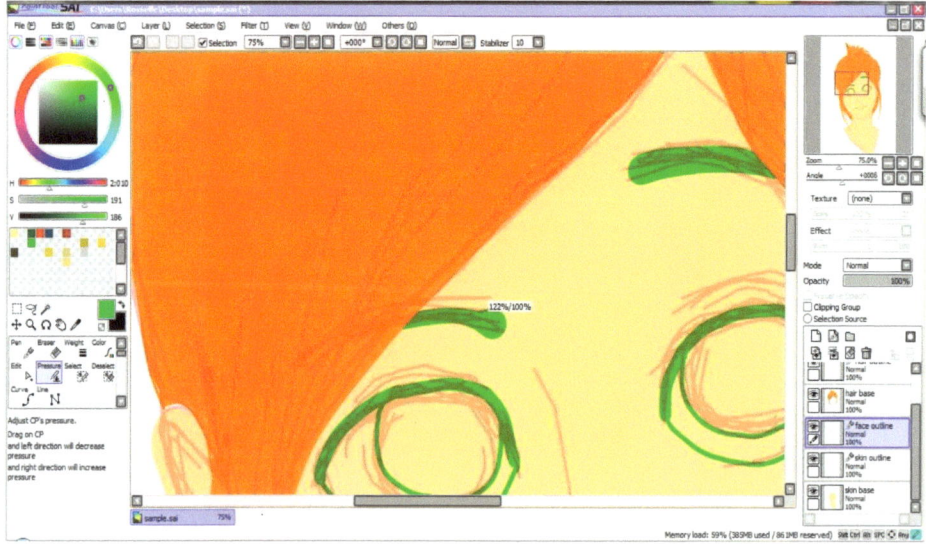

32. This is how the adjusted lines would look like once applied with the Pressure tool. Compare and see how greatly it improved from the previous picture.

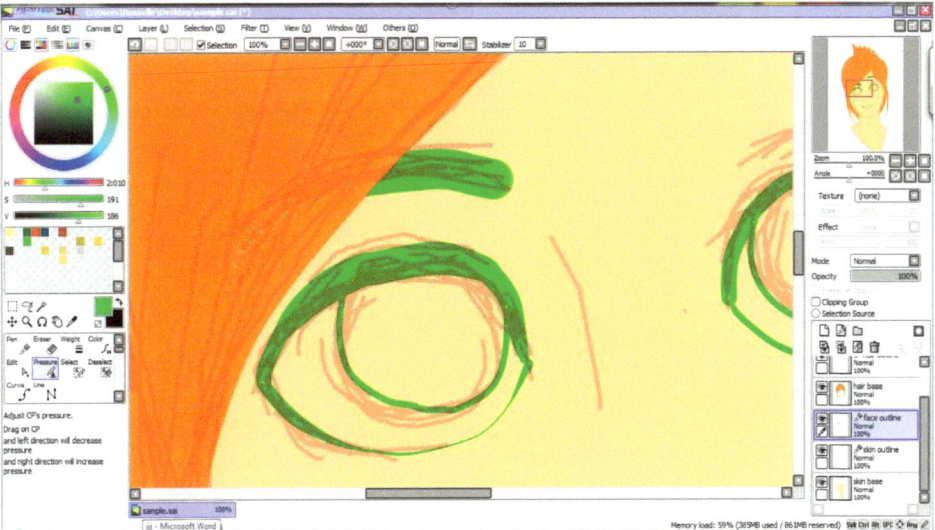

33. This is pretty much how the face would look like.

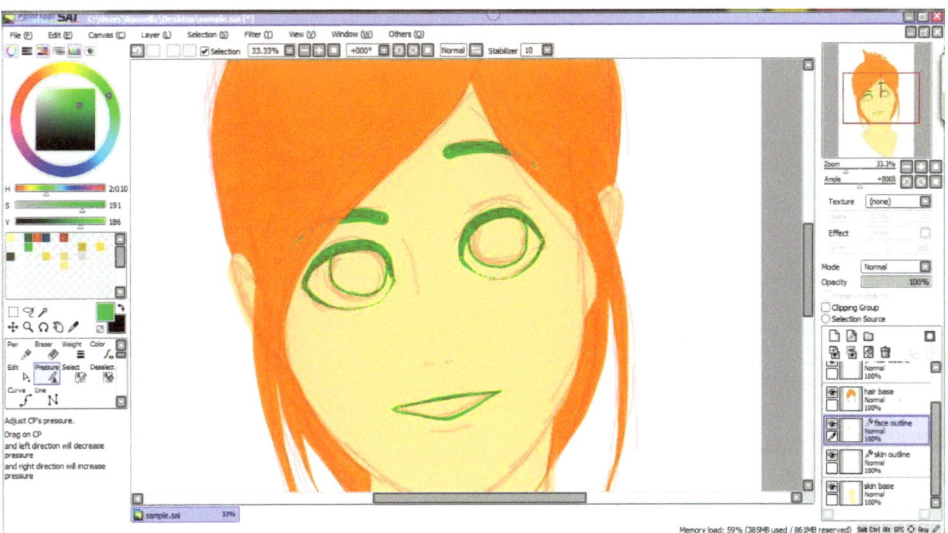

34. Next, I change the color of the eyebrows and the outline of the eye by using the Color tool.

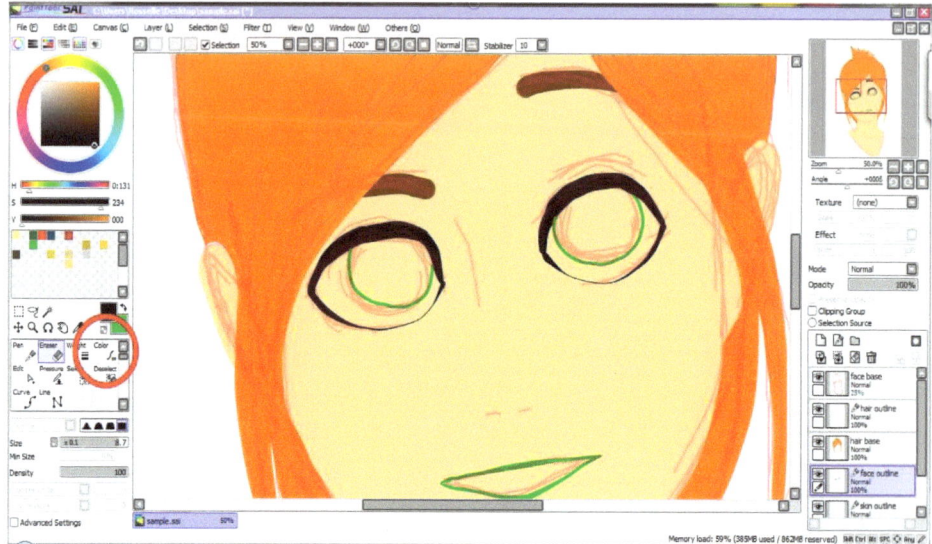

35. Once again, I use the Magic Wand tool to highlight the iris.

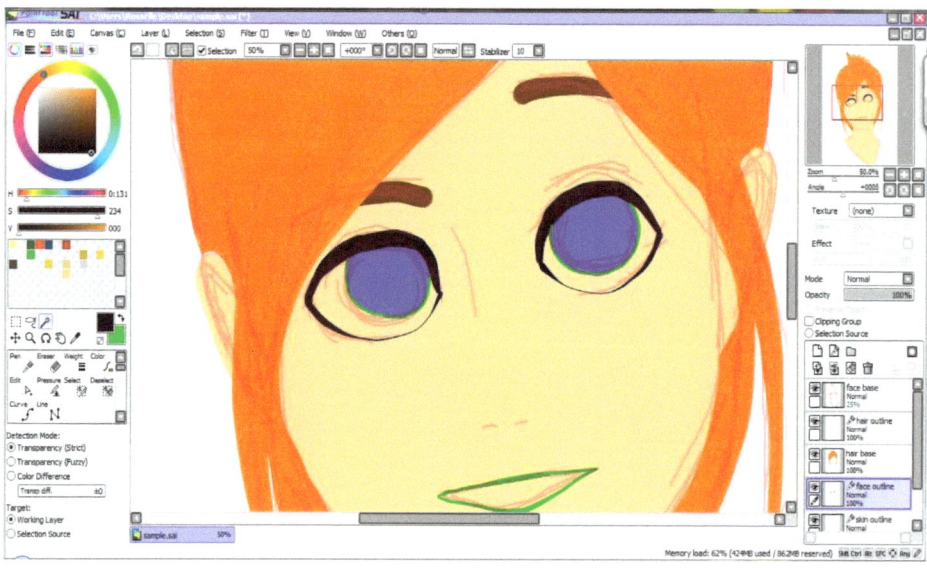

36. I make a new layer for where to put the color of the eyes and label it "eyes base." I repeat the same process to the mouth area.

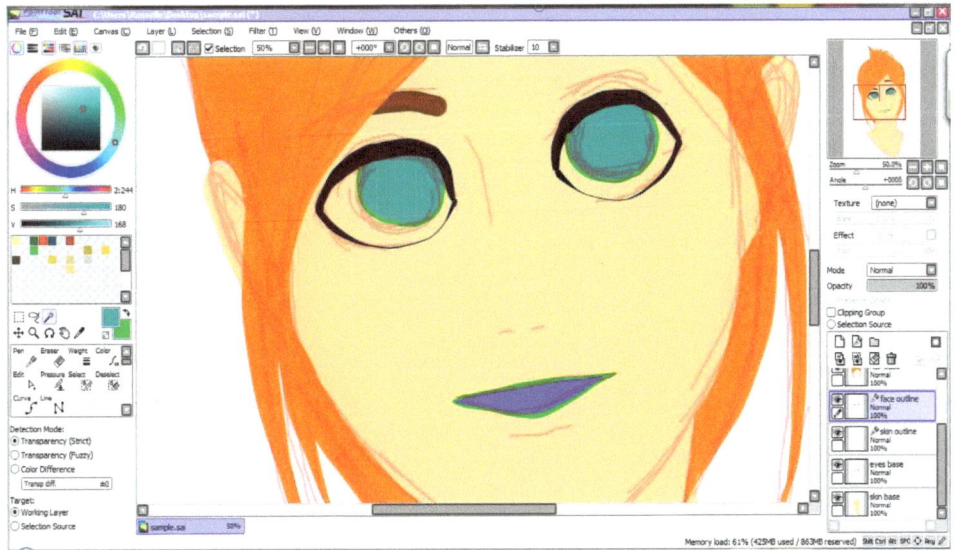

37. I make another layer where I intend to put the coloring of the mouth. Here, I just colored the area white.

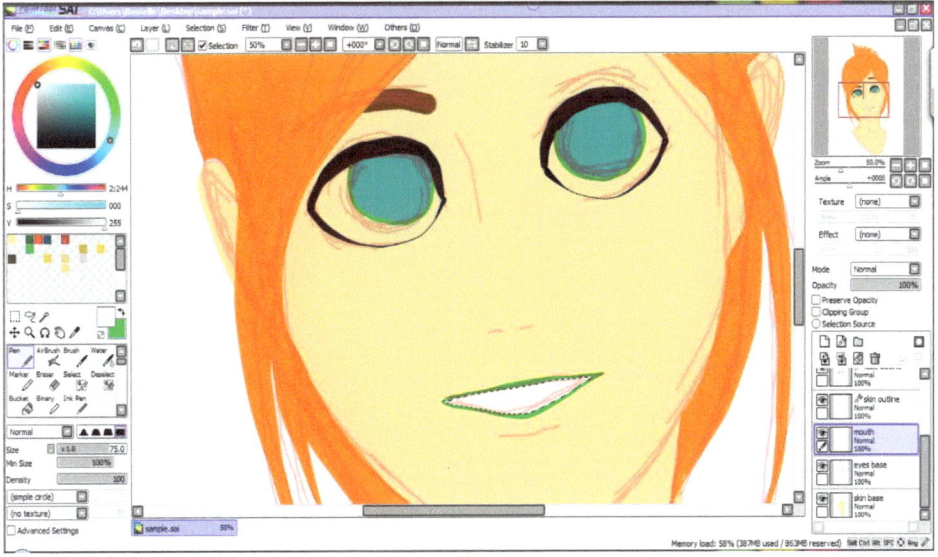

38. I go back to the layer of the Linework of the face to change the color of the outlines.

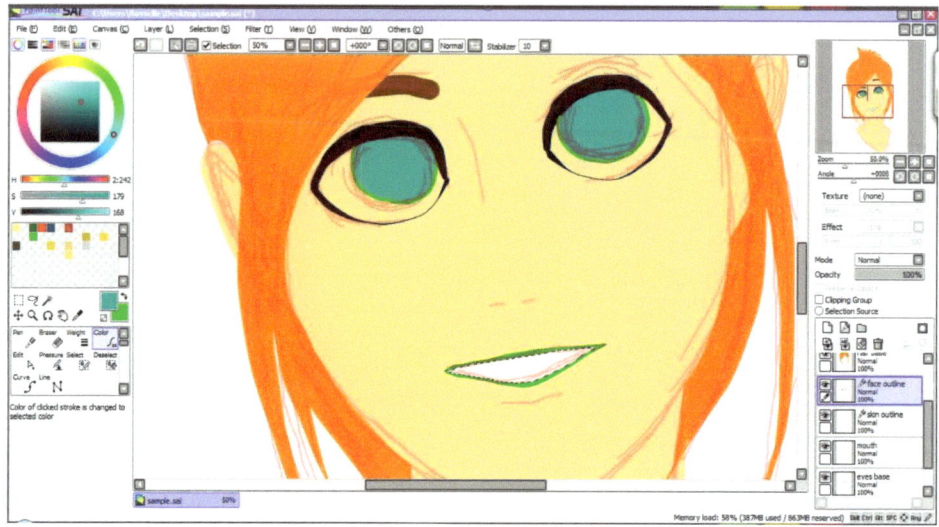

39. I click on the Color tool, and click on the lines with their corresponding color. Now, the upper area is completely colored.

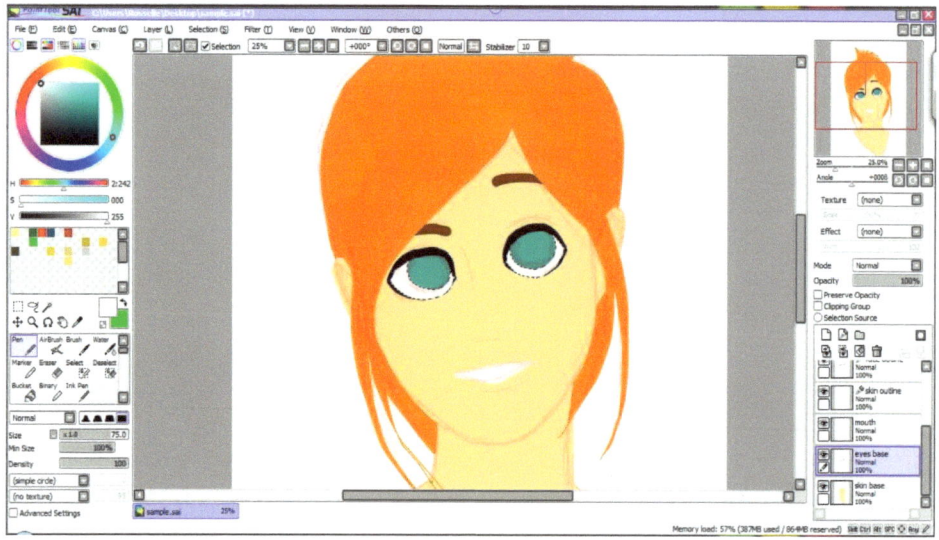

40. Now it's time to make the clothes. Make a new layer and remember to put it above the skin layer.

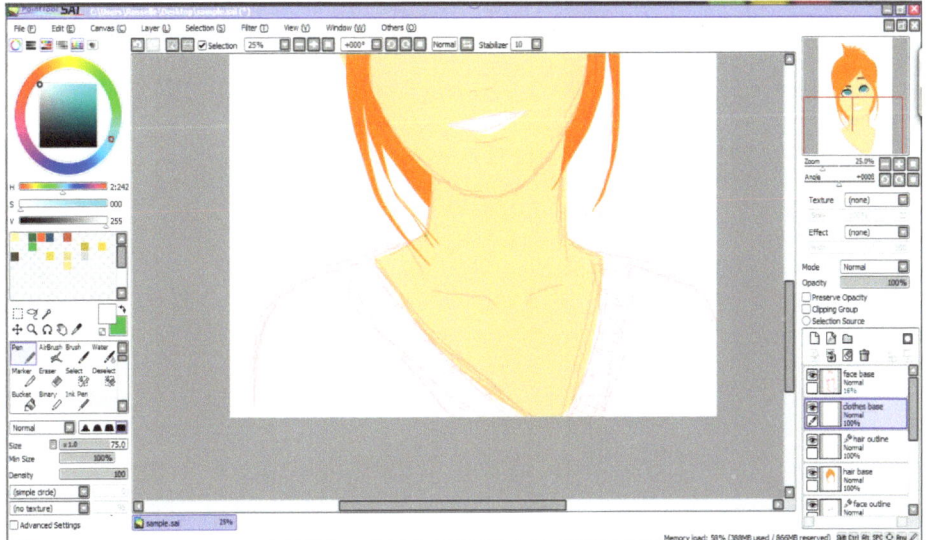

41. I do the sloppy coloring once more.

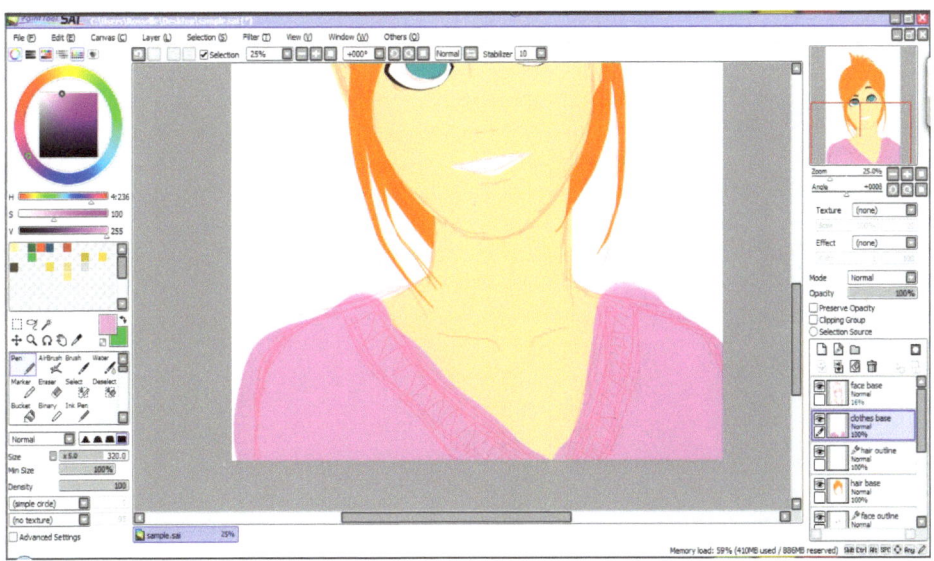

42. Make a new Linework layer for the clothes and proceed to make the outlines.

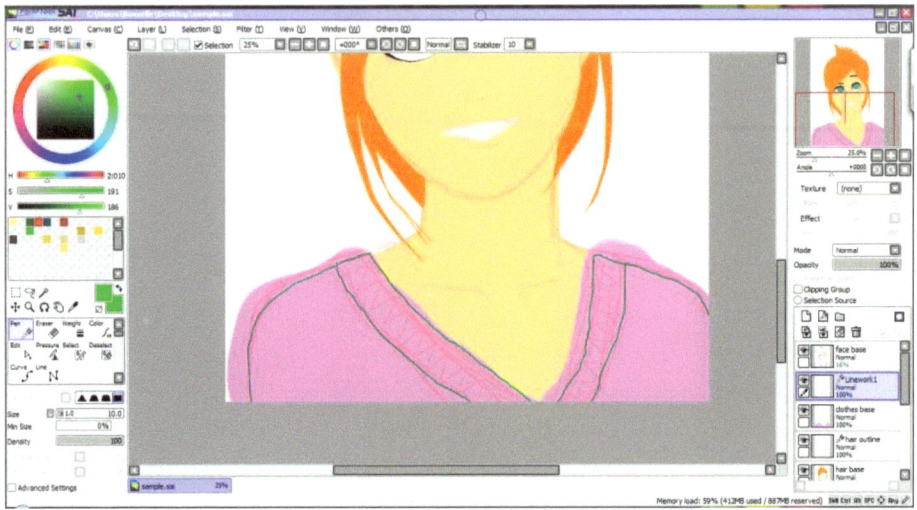

43. Once you have adjusted the lines with the Edit tool, repeat the process of using Magic Wand to highlight the desired area to be colored.

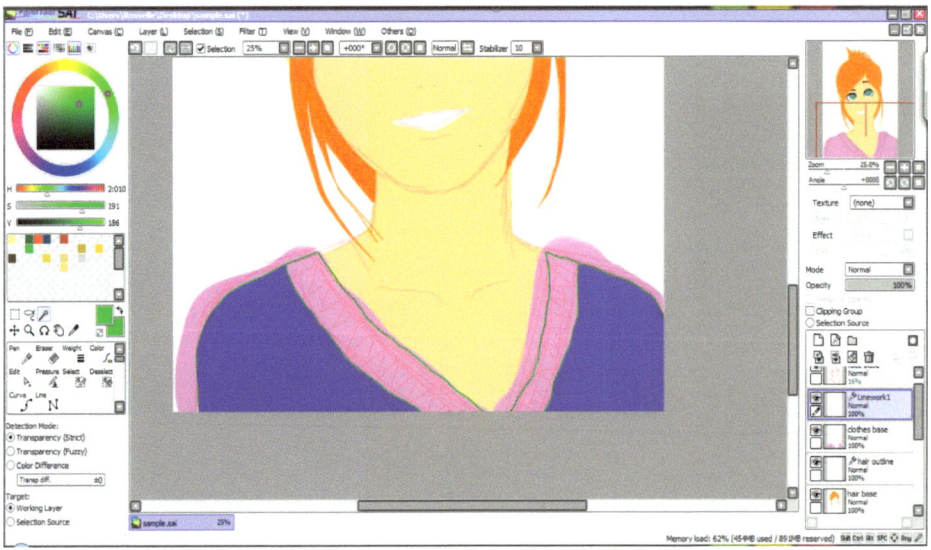

44. Again, invert the selection by clicking the "Selection" button at the top, and choosing "Invert".

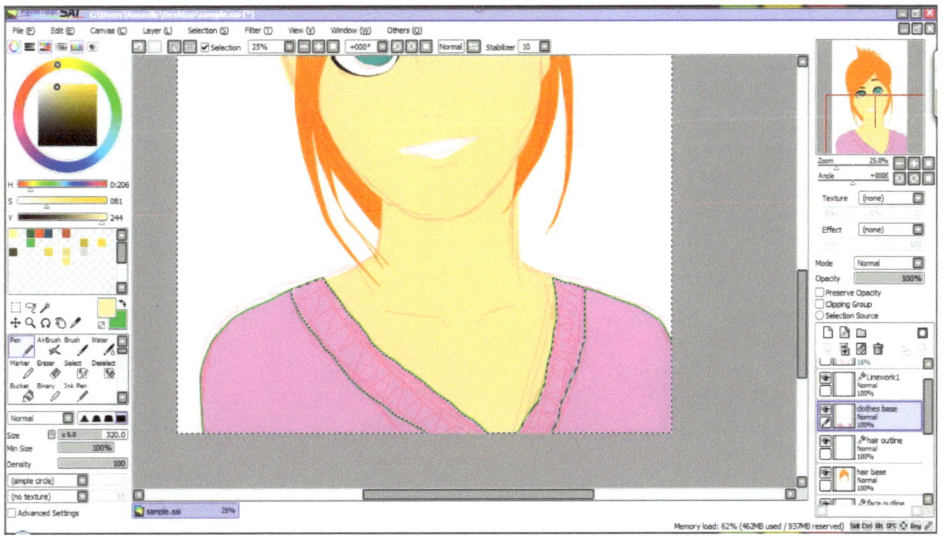

45. Apply the same process to other areas of the clothing that needs to be colored. Always remember to change the color of the lines on the Linework layer to make it fit in with the rest of the coloring.

46. Make a new layer for whatever details you want to put in the clothing. Remember to put it above the base layer where the color of the clothing is.

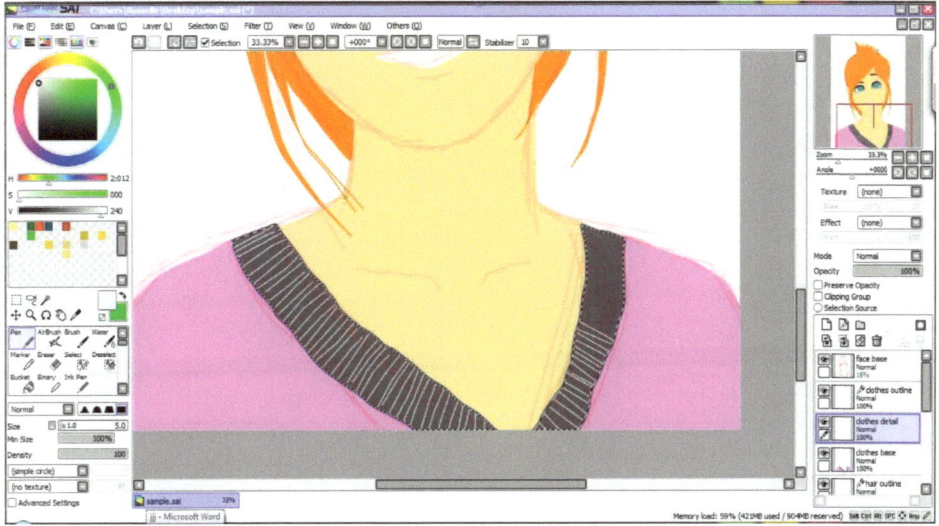

47. This is what the full-colored illustration would look like.

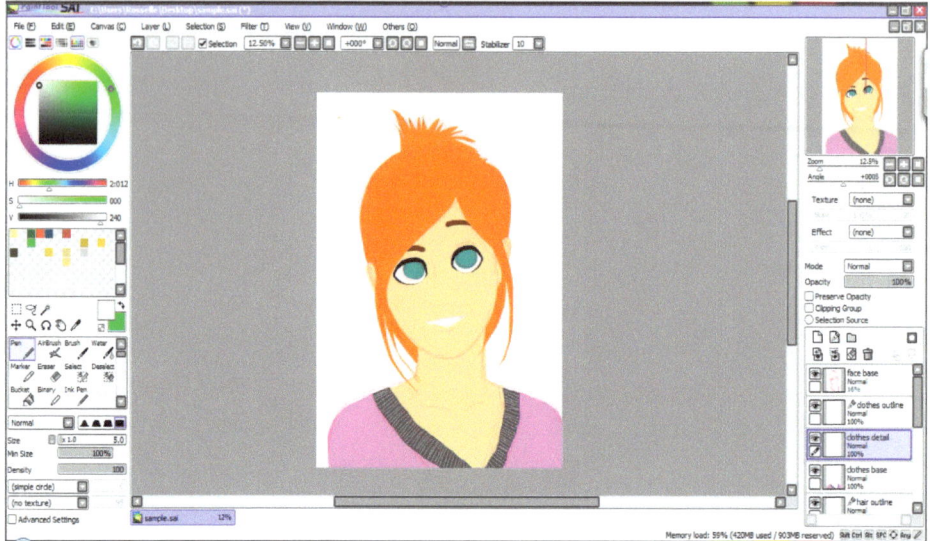

48. Now we move on to shading. First, the neck area. Click on the Linework layer where the outline for the skin is and use the Magic Wand tool. Click on the inside of the skin, as well as the actual line itself. Exclude the facial area first.

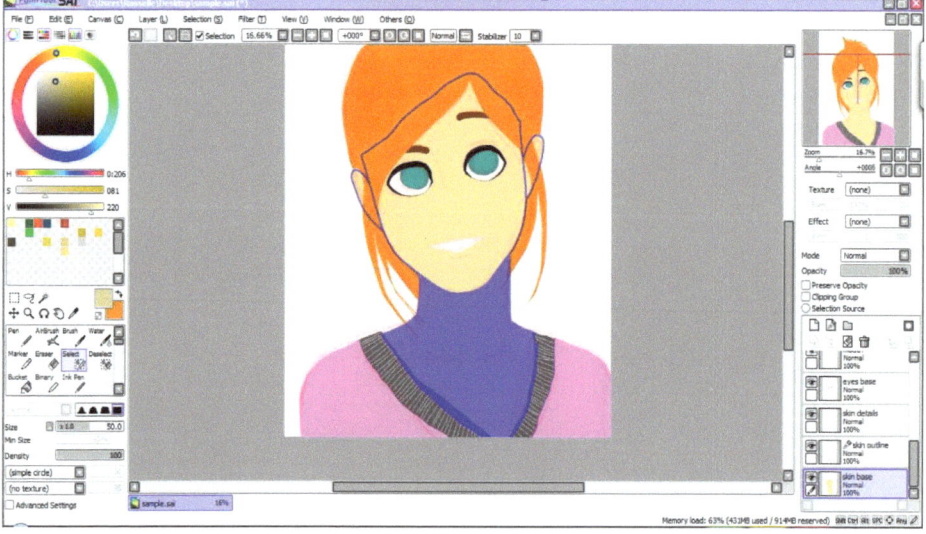

49. I make a new layer for the details of the skin and put it above the layer where the base color of the skin is. I start to make the shadows.

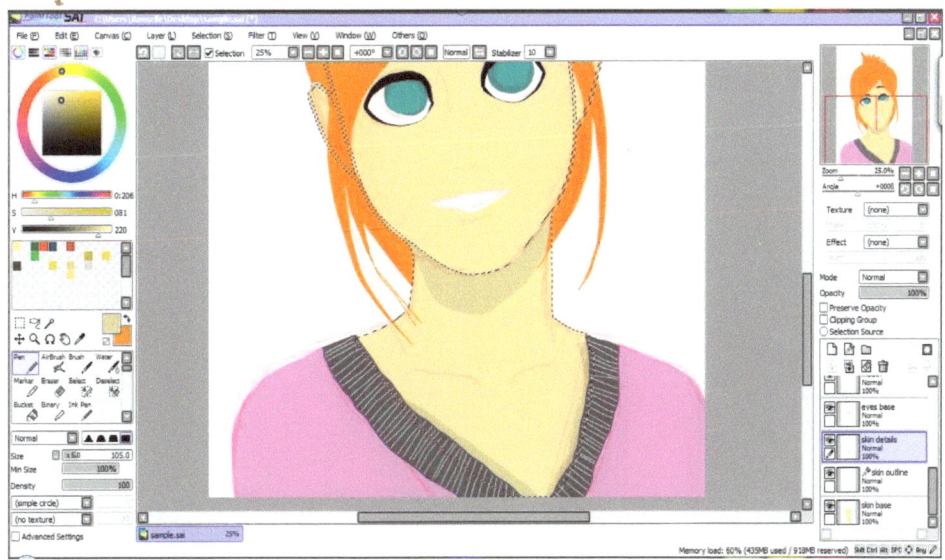

50. I go back to the Linework layer of the skin, now highlighting the facial area, as well as the outline itself.

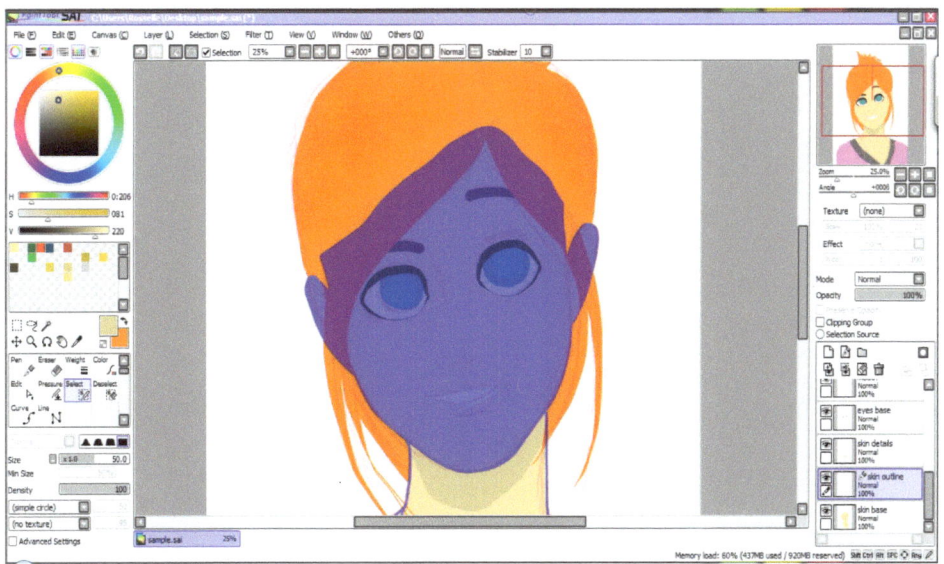

51. On the layer where I put the details of the skin in, I start contouring the face of the subject.

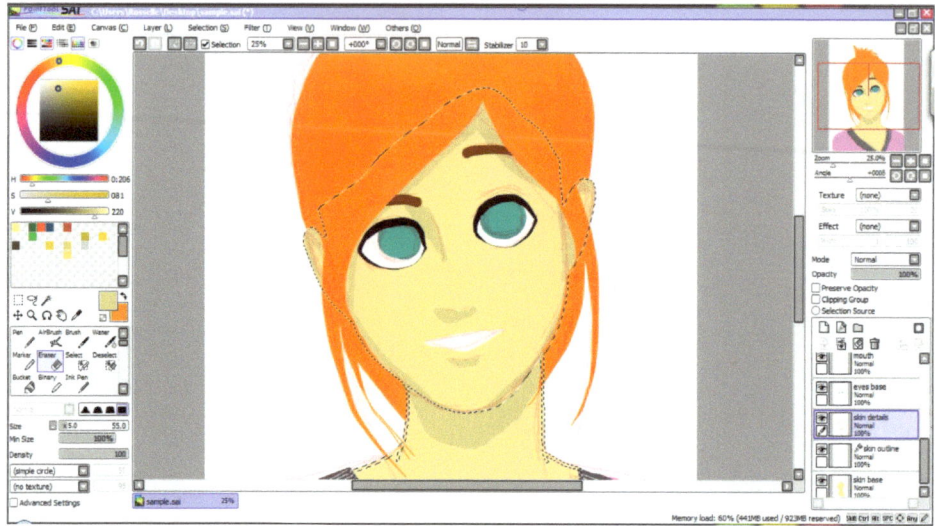

52. Now, since I don't feel the need to see the guide I have made before, I click on the "Show/Hide Layer" button. This is the eye icon right beside the thumbnail of the layer. By clicking this, I make the selected layer invisible.

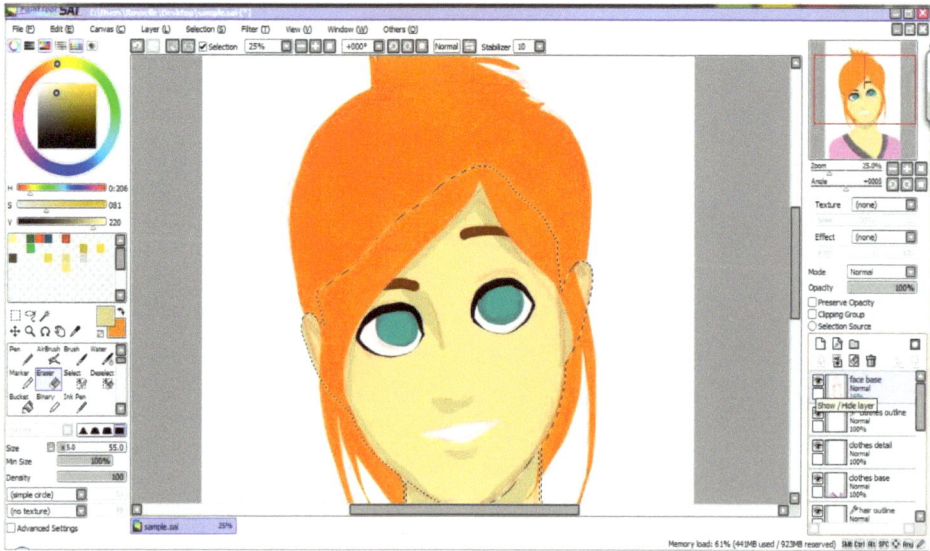

53. Without the faint red lines, I can now see the illustration without any distraction. I proceed to make more contours to the face.

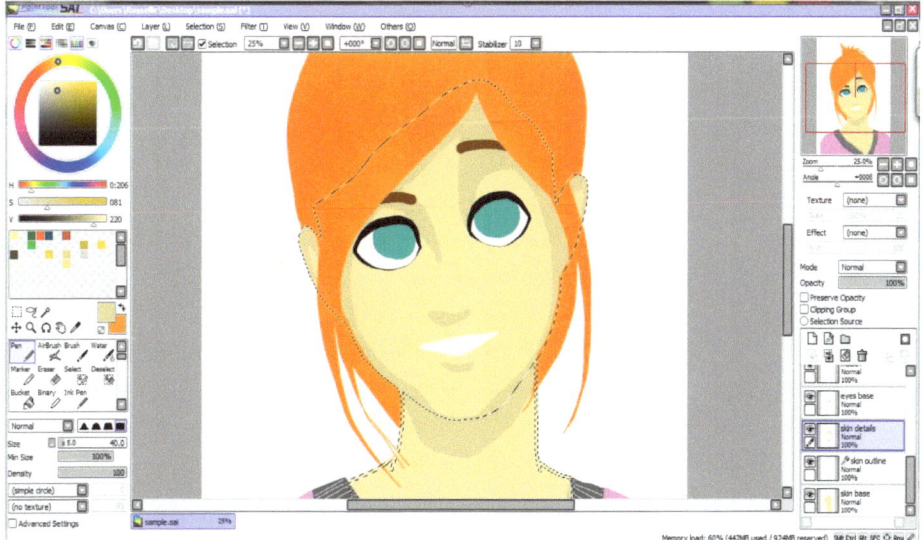

54. Next, I move to shading the hair. I highlight the hair through the Linework layer.

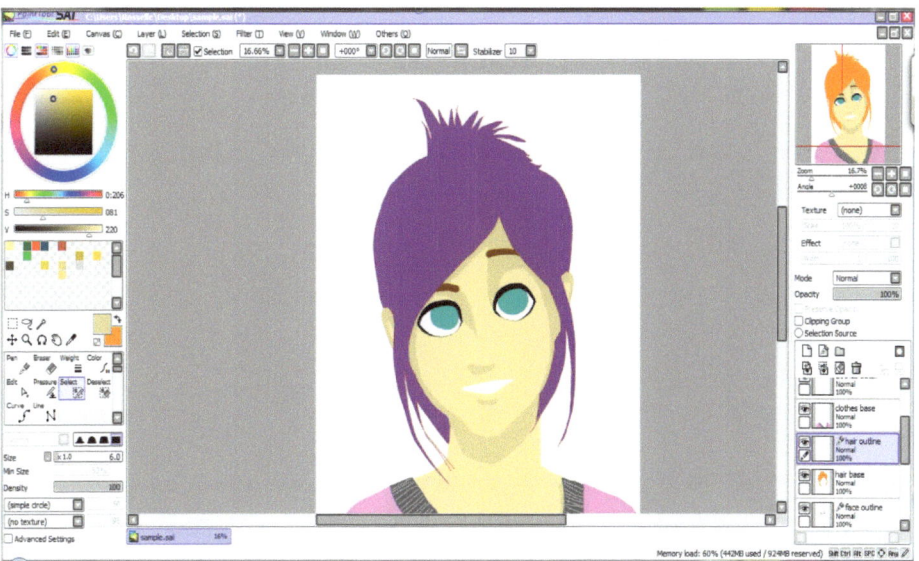

55. I make a new layer for the details of the hair and proceed to add shading.

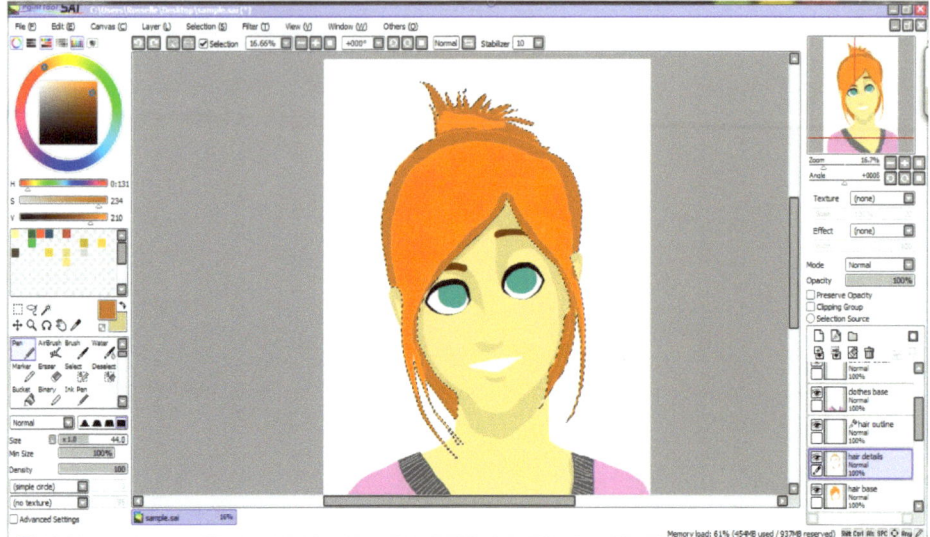

56. Using the Water tool, I blend the dark colors I put in the hair. I changed the "Density" the setting of the said tool so as to make the blending much easier and not seem too plain when looked at.

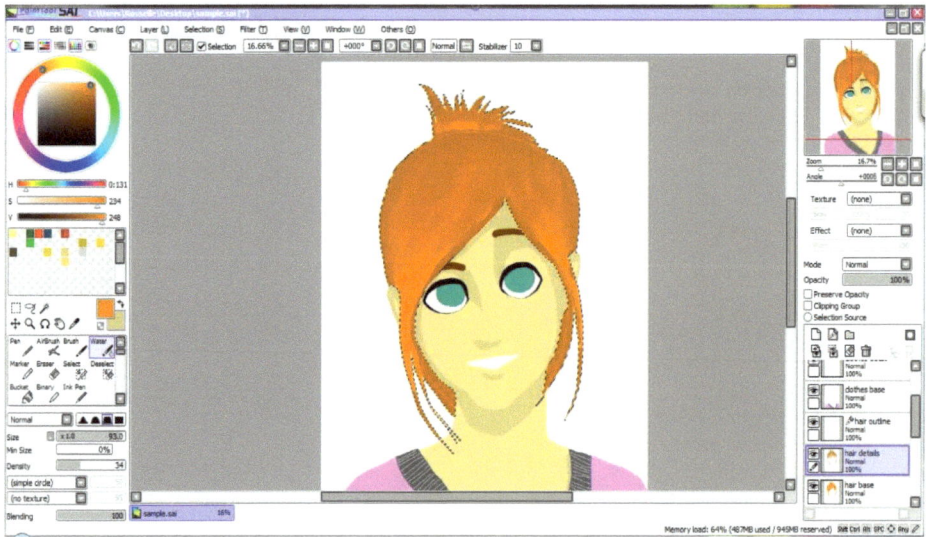

57. I add texture to the hair by making streaks using the thin size of the Pen tool.

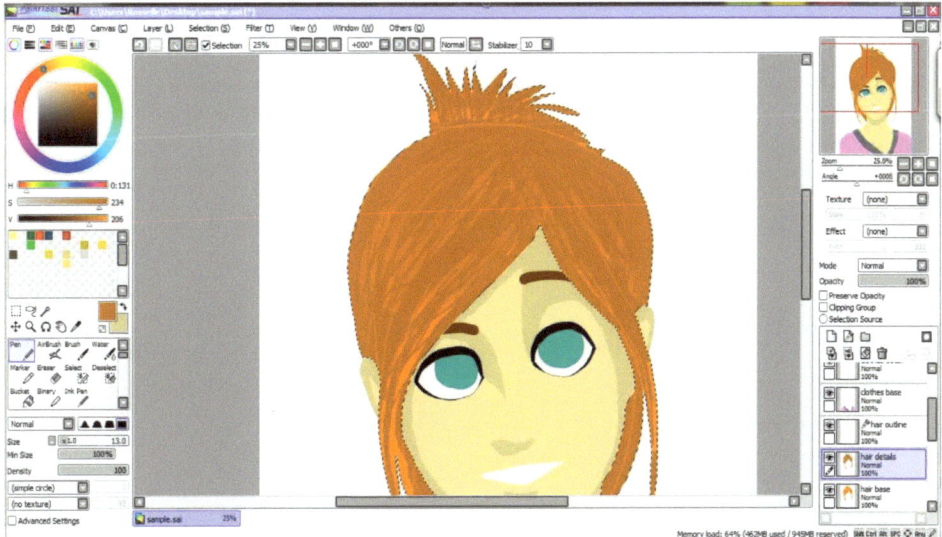

58. Next, I highlight the clothes by using Magic Wand on its outline on the Linework layer.

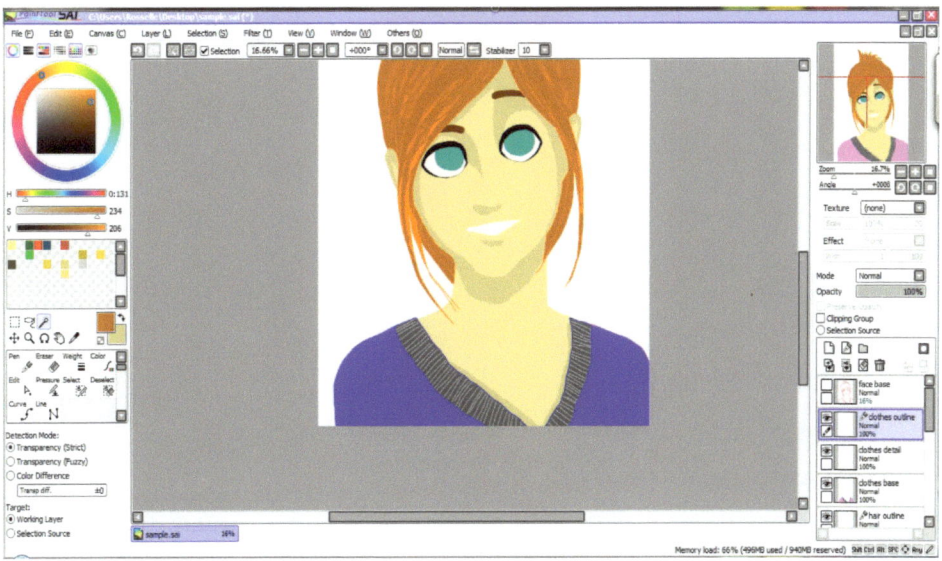

59. I go back to the layer where I put the details of the clothes. On this, I added shading to it.

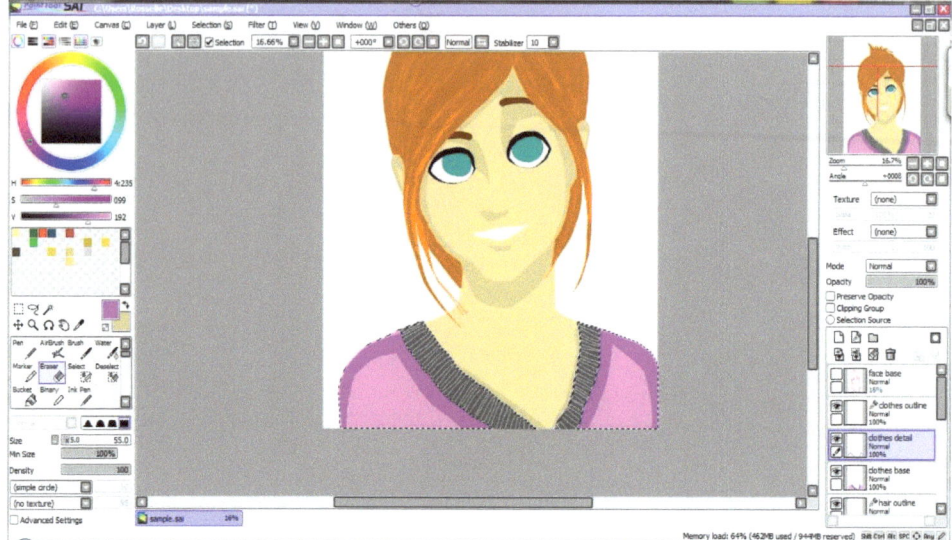

60. Once again, I applied the Water tool to blend the colors.

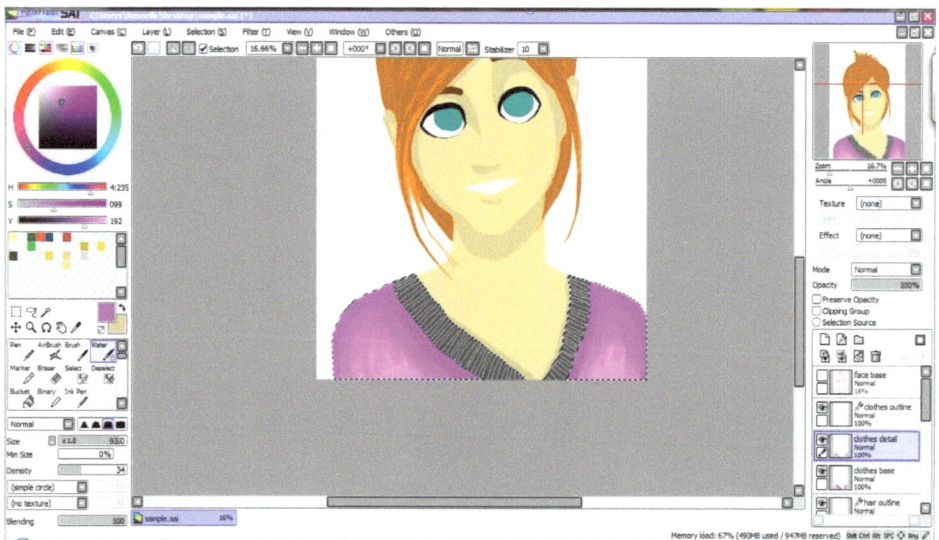

61. On the layer where I put in the base color of the eyes, I added a white circle to depict the reflection of light.

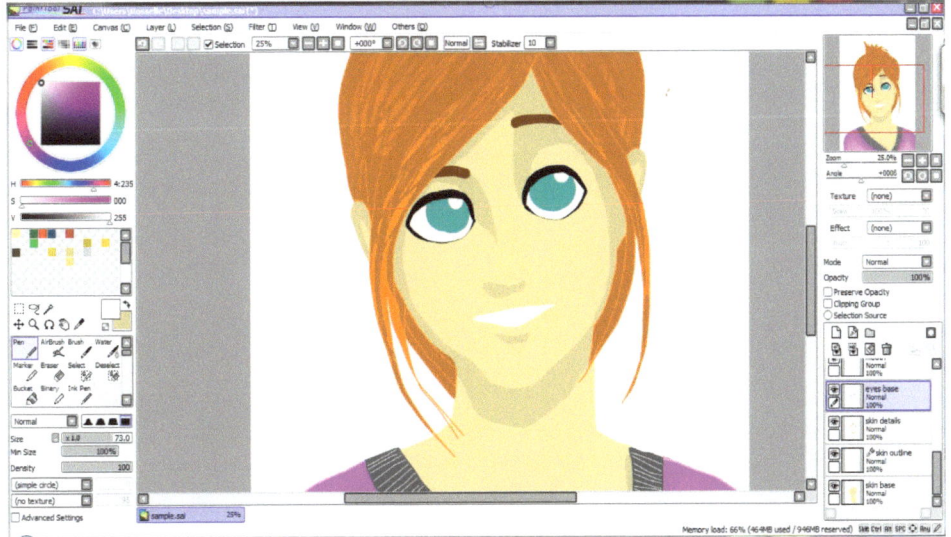

62. I apply Water tool to the contours of the face to soften its look.

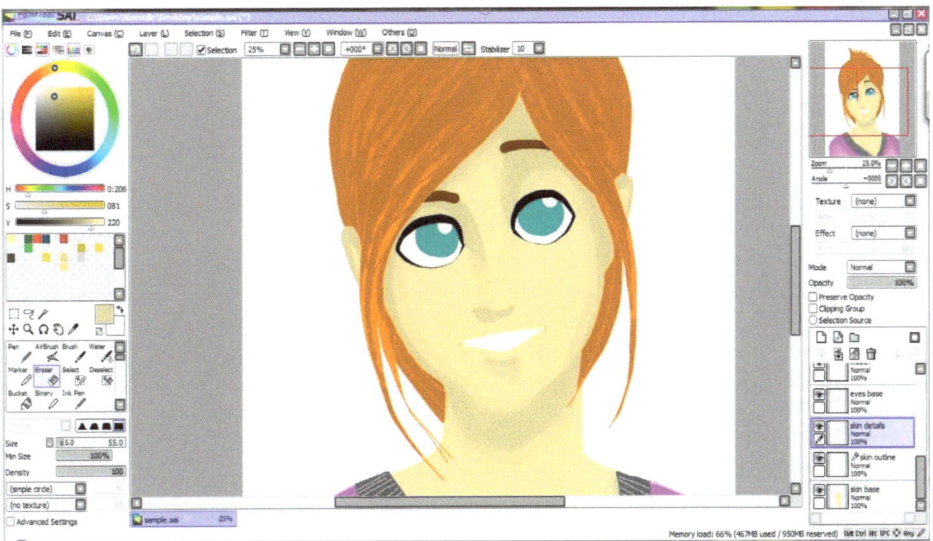

63. I used Water tool on the hair and added a few light spots to add texture. I also used the Pen tool in its very, very small size to add loose strands of hair, giving her a slightly messy look.

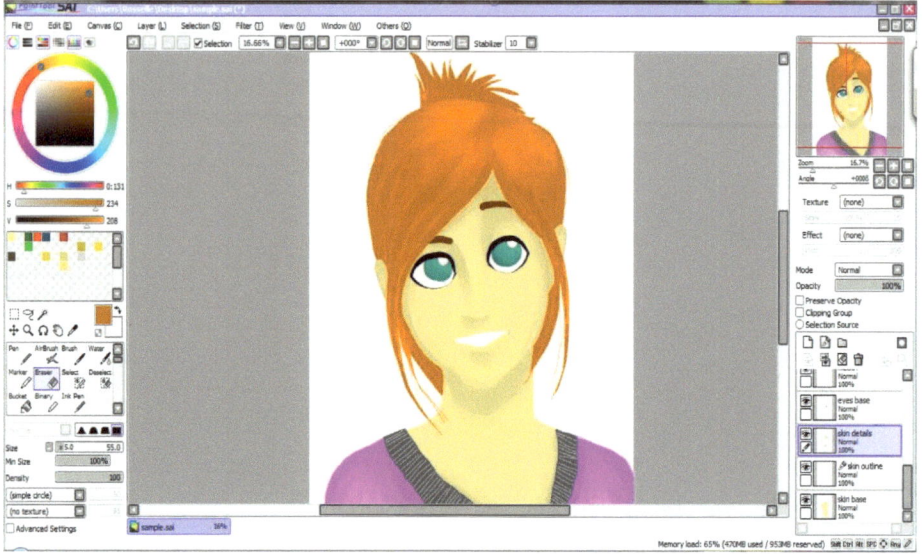

64. I gave it a background color by putting a new layer at the bottommost part and applying the Bucket tool. Simply click on the canvas and whatever color is selected from the palette will instantly be the background color.

And I'm done!

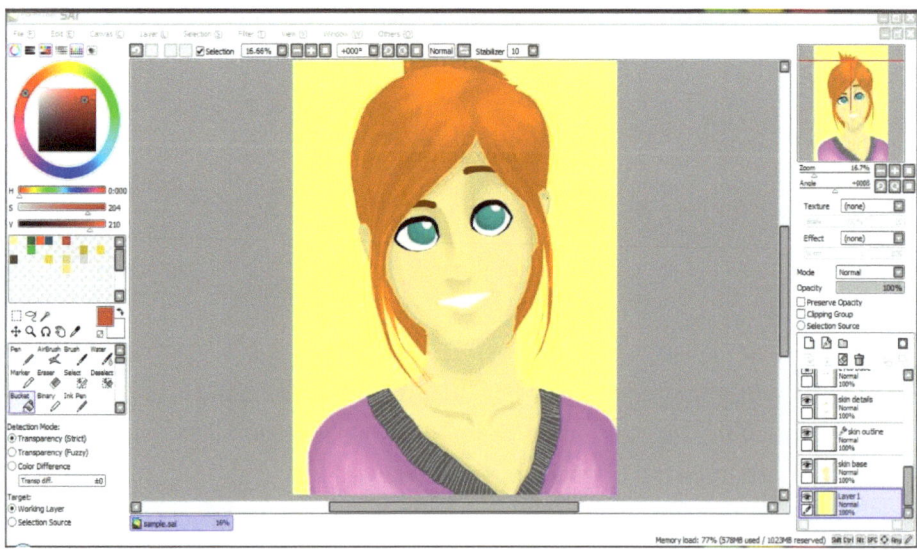

STUFF TO REMEMBER:

- When drafting, it's always better to use a very vibrant color of the Pen/Pencil tool to avoid confusion in the coloring process.

- Lowering the opacity of the finished draft greatly helps in the coloring process.

- On **Layers**:

  > Always rename the new layer you're working on. This would save you a lot of time in the long run.

  > It's better to have made a lot of layers than to accidentally alter content that doesn't need to be.

  > What you put on top is what would be readily seen. What you put at the bottom would be the background of it.

- On **Linework**:

  > One of the main purposes of making a Linework layer is for the utilization of the Magic Wand tool when it comes to coloring. Hence, it would only work if you make the lines form a closed figure.

  > You can always use the Edit tool for literally any point on the line you have made. Don't be too wary of making mistakes.

  > You can change the color of an entire line by the Color tool. By clicking on the line with the desired replacement color selected on the color palette, the line will change its color instantly.

  > Using the Pressure tool is a great help, especially to those who utilize *visible outlines* (unlike my style) on their drawings. To thicken a segment, drag the highlighted point to the left. To make a segment thin, drag the highlighted point to the right.

- For the nth time, don't be afraid to make mistakes! After all, this is all digital and each step can be undone with just a simple "Ctrl"+"Z".

- Experiment. There's no greater teacher than experience. See how each tool differs from one another. Observe the approach of different artists when it comes to outlines and colors. Remember that the learning process is continuous--there's always something out there waiting to be discovered and learned.

• Converting to digital drawing takes a lot of adjustments, so it's very easy to be demoralized when you're starting. Always remember that drawing on a tablet needs some getting used to, so be easy on yourself.

• Practice. Becoming adept in digital drawing doesn't come instantly--I know in my case that it didn't. It took a long time of practice, observation, as well as tremendous frustrations before I can finally say that I have gotten the flow of it.

• Don't forget that art is supposed to be an enjoyable experience to the artist. Love what you do, and with perseverance, you'd be amazed yourself at how far you've gone.

Author Bio

Rosselle Taruc is currently a Communications student in Manila, Philippines. She has been drawing ever since she discovered that friction between the tip of a pencil and a piece of paper magically produces lines. When she's feeling brave, she occasionally posts stuff she drew, poems she wrote, and thoughts she yap about on Tumblr, where she goes by *potatocrayon*. She lives with her family and their 9 goldfishes.

Check out our other books

Learn To Draw Series

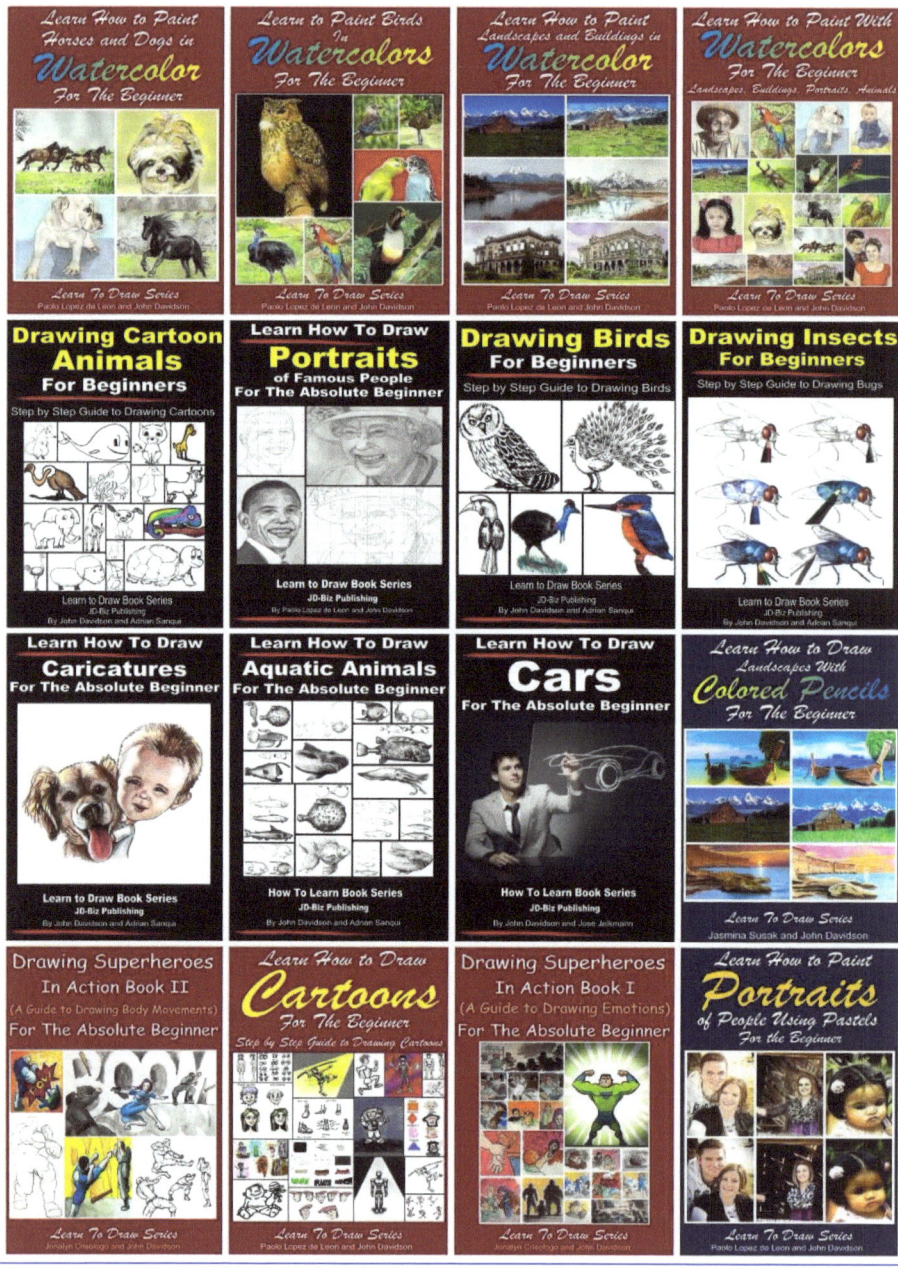

Our books are available at

1. Amazon.com

2. Barnes and Noble

3. Itunes

4. Kobo

5. Smashwords

6. Google Play Books

Publisher

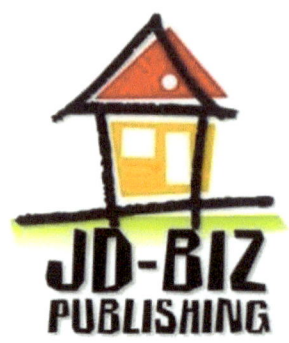

JD-Biz Corp

P O Box 374

Mendon, Utah 84325

http://www.jd-biz.com/

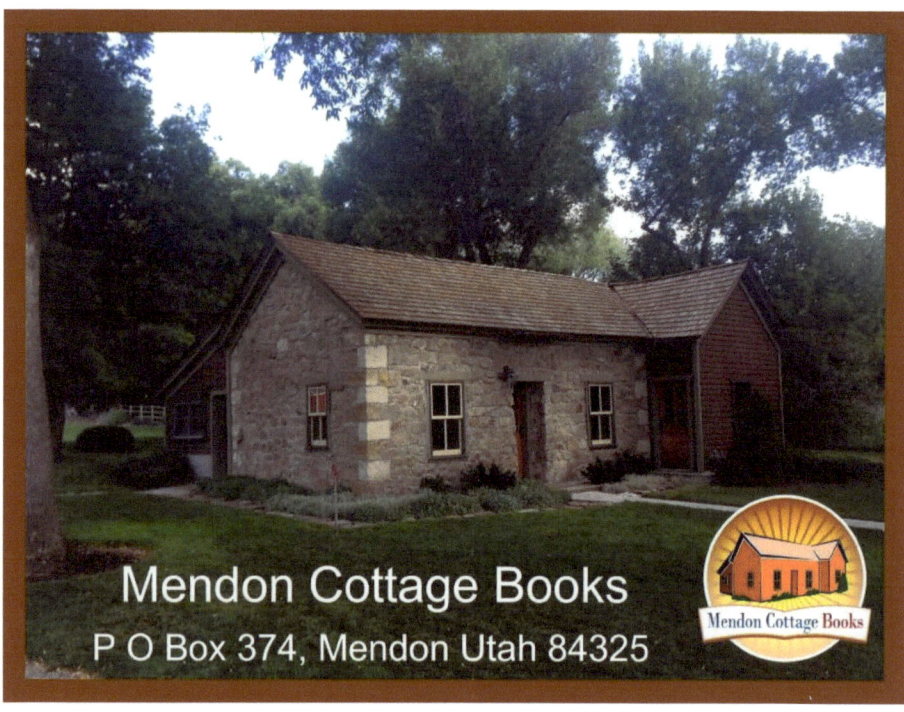